Warrior • 29

Ashigaru 1467–1649

Stephen Turnbull · Illustrated by Howard Gerrard

First published in Great Britain in 2001 by Osprey Publishing,
Midland House, West Way, Botley, Oxford OX2 0PH, UK
443 Park Avenue South, New York, NY 10016, USA
Email: info@ospreypublishing.com

CIP Data for this publication is available from the British Library

ISBN 978 1 84176 149 7

Editor: Marcus Cowper
Design: Alan Hamp
Originated by PPS Grasmere Ltd, Leeds, UK
Printed in China through World Print Ltd.
Typeset in Helvetica Neue and ITC New Baskerville

07 08 09 10 11 12 11 10 9 8 7 6 5 4 3

FOR A CATALOGUE OF ALL BOOKS PUBLISHED BY OSPREY
MILITARY AND AVIATION PLEASE CONTACT:

NORTH AMERICA
Osprey Direct, C/o Random House Distribution Center,
400 Hahn Road, Westminster, MD 21157, USA
E-mail: info@ospreydirect.com

ALL OTHER REGIONS
Osprey Direct UK, P.O. Box 140, Wellingborough, Northants, NN8 2FA, UK
E-mail: info@ospreydirect.co.uk

Buy online at **www.ospreypublishing.com**

Dedication

To Janet Arrowsmith

Preface and Acknowledgements

To the popular view, the only warriors of Japan were 'the samurai',
proud, individual mounted knights, whose goal in life was to serve
their lord with unswerving devotion, seeking out on the battlefield a
worthy opponent whose severed head would provide the finest and
most dramatic proof of their loyalty. This was the samurai ideal,
nurtured by the re-telling of the deeds of their ancestors, whose
exploits grew in stature as the centuries went by.

Yet throughout Japanese history the elite samurai were always
backed up in various ways by numerous lower-class footsoldiers.
Conscripted farmers, loyal attendants on samurai or absconding
peasants all fulfilled the role of footsoldier, but their deeds went
largely unrecognised and unrecorded until a major convulsion in
Japanese society gave them a new prominence and new worth.
Change arrived with the beginning of the *Sengoku-jidai*, the 'Period
of Warring States', which lasted from AD 1467 to 1615. The term,
which is taken from the Chinese dynastic histories, reflects the
fact that centralised authority had collapsed and the *daimyô*,
the equivalent of European feudal lords, fought each other
for supremacy.

The new breed of footsoldiers were called ashigaru, a word that
literally means 'light feet'. At the core of what was to become a new
infantry arm in Japanese warfare were the part-time soldier/farmers
who had served the daimyô for generations, but, as the demand for
fighting men grew, their numbers were swelled by hundreds of
casual and opportunistic ne'er-do-wells, attracted to army life by
the prospect of loot. As time went by they began to stay with a
particular daimyô and merged with the men who already worked on
the daimyô's lands and served him in battle. The ashigaru's final
stage of development was their emergence as experienced
operators of sophisticated weaponry in disciplined squads wearing
identical uniforms, whose use on the battlefield complemented that
of the mounted samurai.

In compiling this account of the ashigaru I have been helped by
numerous individuals and organisations. Except where other credits
are noted, the pictures from *Ehon Taikôki*, *Zôhyô Monogatari* and
Ehon Toyotomi Gunki are from private collections, and *Geijutsu
Hiden Zue* is reproduced by courtesy of the Royal Armouries
Museum, Leeds.

I would particularly like to thank Thom Richardson and Ian
Bottomley of the Royal Armouries Museum, Leeds; Yoko Fujino of
the Watanabe Museum, Tottori; Yoshiko Sakamoto of Osaka Castle
Museum; and Mr Noboru Koyama of Cambridge University Library
for their advice and help. My greatest thanks, as always, are to my
own family.

Artist's Note

Readers may care to note that the original paintings from which the
colour plates in this book were prepared are available for private
sale. All reproduction copyright whatsoever is retained by the
Publishers. All enquiries should be addressed to:

Howard Gerrard, 11 Oaks Road, Tenterden, Kent TN30 6RD, UK

The Publishers regret that they can enter into no correspondence
upon this matter.

ASHIGARU 1467–1649

THE ASHIGARU: A HISTORICAL SURVEY

THE ANTECEDENTS OF the ashigaru may be traced to one of the earliest attempts by a Japanese emperor to control and systematise the owning and use of military force. To this end, Emperor Tenmu (reigned 673-86) envisaged a national army that was to consist largely of conscripted footsoldiers, but as they often absconded from duty the programme was eventually abandoned. By the 10th century the government began instead to rely on the military service provided by the landowning classes, whose possession of horses had already guaranteed their position as the 'officer class' of the conscript armies. These men were the first samurai, who were supported in their endeavours by scores of lower class troops who at other times worked on the land. Some footsoldiers had long connections with a particular family or geographical area, and would tend to act in the capacity of genin (warrior's attendant). They would carry a samurai's equipment or act as grooms, and would also perform the important function of collecting the severed heads, each of which counted to their master's total. The genin would fight if necessary, particularly if the samurai's life was in danger, but samurai combat was largely regarded as a private duel in which the rival genin provided only

The scroll *Heiji Monogatari Emaki* shows better than any other contemporary illustration the class distinction between mounted samurai and footsoldiers in Japan during the Gempei Wars. A rough looking footsoldier (centre right) with an *eboshi* cap carries a severed head on his *naginata*. He has bare legs. The mounted samurai wear much more elaborate armour, and are painted as possessing a greater delicacy of breeding. (Courtesy of the Museum of Fine Arts, Boston)

a supportive function. Their service was valued nonetheless, and loyal genin occasionally received promotion to samurai status.

In a typical army there were other footsoldiers, however, to whom such ties of social obligation and personal service were either weak or non-existent. These men were often hastily recruited, badly trained and poorly armed. To the compilers of the epic chronicles of samurai warfare, they were almost invisible and invariably anonymous, and it is only through careful reading of the texts that their presence on the battlefield becomes apparent. Curiously, the neglect of the footsoldier in the written accounts of battle is not to be found in the artistic works, such as scroll paintings and screens, which have survived from these times. The *Heiji Monogatari Emaki*, for example, includes numerous vignettes of soldiers who fight on foot. The artist has clearly taken great pains to show the contrast between the footsoldiers and the elite mounted samurai, whose armour is more extensive and more elaborate. In physical appearance too, the footsoldiers are painted as coarse, rough characters, with whiskered faces, and with a noticeable lack of delicacy compared to their betters. Other examples show the contrast between samurai and footsoldiers in terms of the functions they perform. The samurai demonstrate prowess at mounted archery, while the mob of footsoldiers set fire to buildings.

In the Gempei Wars (1180-85), the Minamoto family triumphed over their rivals the Taira, and the first *Shogun* – the military dictator whose power eclipsed that of the emperor – was appointed. Yet wars still continued, with footsoldiers appearing occasionally in the accounts as either combatants or victims. For example, in the chronicle *Azuma Kagami* for 1221 we read:

'Eastern warriors filled the neighbouring provinces, seeking out footsoldiers who had fled the battlefields. Heads rolled constantly, naked blades were wiped over and over.'

A wounded footsoldier falls to the floor with an arrow protruding from his eye socket. From the *Kasuga Gongen genki e*. (Courtesy of the Imperial Household collection)

A simple forehead and face protector, as worn by foot-soldiers of the 12th century.

The rise of ashigaru

In 1274 and 1281 elite samurai, supported by footsoldiers, drove back the two Mongol invasions. Japan then enjoyed many years of comparative peace until an ill-fated attempt at imperial restoration led to the Nanbokucho Wars, which were fought in the name of two rival emperors and lasted for much of the 14th century. Many of the actions of these wars were fought from defended positions in mountainous areas, and a new way of using archery was developed. Instead of single arrows being fired at targets by elite mounted samurai, huge volleys of arrows were launched into the enemy ranks by footsoldiers, a technique that had been used against the Japanese by the Mongols. The *Taiheiki* refers to these lower-class archers as *shashu no ashigaru* (ashigaru shooters), the first use of the term 'ashigaru' in Japanese history. Out of 2,000 men who fought for the Sasaki at the battle of Shijo Nawate in 1348 800 were these 'light archers'.

A century later the word 'ashigaru' appears again in the different context of the disastrous Ônin War of 1467-77, a particularly savage conflict which was fought mainly around Kyoto, the capital city, whose wealth provided endless opportunities for looting, arson and extortion. Kyoto was the seat of the Shogun, but as his power declined so that of the daimyô grew. These petty warlords needed fighting men, and for a landless peasant dissatisfied with his lot the lawlessness of the times offered a sellers' market. The name 'ashigaru' (light feet) indicated their lack of armour, footwear, or even weaponry until all three were looted from a defeated enemy. Such men found it easy to attach themselves casually to samurai armies, and then fight, pillage and ultimately desert.

An ambitious daimyô was therefore able to increase the numbers of his footsoldiers tenfold by the addition of such a loose and uncertain rabble. Unfortunately, it often turned out that men who had been casually recruited would just as easily disappear to till the fields and swell the armies of an enemy. Untrained peasants attracted only by personal gain were also not the ideal candidates to fight in organised groups and wield increasingly sophisticated weapons. There was therefore a need for continuity, for the development of skills, and above all for the inculcation of the loyalty that was already expected from the daimyô's own men. Both these trends developed as the Period of Warring States continued and battles, sieges and campaigns grew larger in scale.

The final conclusion was a recognition that, although the ashigaru, whatever their origin, were different from the elite samurai, their fighting skills could be complementary. The successful daimyô was one who used footsoldiers in a combination of arms, controlled by samurai, but who valued the contribution they could make toward victory.

Ashigaru earn armour

Evidence of the increasingly important role of ashigaru is found in the numerous surviving suits of armour made for them. Known simply as *okashi gusoku* (loan armour), ashigaru armour was of plain construction, consisting of little more than a *dô* (body armour) with *kusazuri* (skirts), together with a simple helmet called a *jingasa* (war hat). The existence of such armour shows that the daimyô, who provided them, now valued the service of the ashigaru sufficiently to give them armour rather than

5

expecting them to turn up with their own. Also, nearly all okashi gusoku had the daimyô's *mon* (badge) stencilled on the front of the dô. A simple heraldic device was sometimes additionally carried on an identifying *sashimono* (flag) flying from the rear of the ashigaru's armour. Some, notably the Ii clan from Hikone, dressed all their troops in the same coloured armour. The combined effect of these moves was to transform the ashigaru costume into a military uniform.

Improved military status, however, would only arrive with a change in the choice of weaponry allocated to the ashigaru. During the heroic days of the Gempei Wars (1180-85) the primary samurai weapon was the bow, and prowess at archery was the most prized samurai accomplishment. Yet by about 1530 we see ashigaru used regularly as missile troops while the mounted samurai fight with spears rather than bows. From the 1550s onwards the ashigaru bows were augmented by firearms, but for these to be effective they had to be placed at the front of an army, the position traditionally occupied by the most loyal and glorious samurai. There was much honour attached to being the first to come to grips with an enemy. To place the lowest ranking troops in such a position was a challenge to samurai pride, even allowing for an overall tactical plan that envisaged the ashigaru's fire merely breaking down enemy ranks ready for a spirited charge by samurai, at which point the ashigaru politely held back. Yet by the 1590s such troop arrangements had become commonplace, showing a profound difference in military attitude. Not everyone approved, and there exists a scornful comment in a later chronicle which laments that instead of ten or 20 horsemen riding out together from an army's ranks, there is now only this thing called 'ashigaru warfare'.

From the time of the Ônin War between 1467 and 1477 the power of the Shogun declined, and samurai warlords began to assert their independence. This provided the opportunity for peasants to join armies on a casual basis, and such men were the original ashigaru. In this illustration from *Ehon Toyotomi Gunki* a group of farmers are seen in a warlike mood; however, they are armed only with one spear, converted agricultural implements and a bamboo pole.

Nobunaga shows the way forward

The new trend was given a dramatic illustration in 1575 with Oda Nobunaga's victory at the battle of Nagashino. Nobunaga, who was faced by the prospect of a devastating cavalry charge against him by the renowned samurai of the Takeda clan, lined up all his arquebus squads into three ranks protected by a loose palisade. Under the iron discipline of his most experienced samurai the ashigaru gunners fired controlled volleys into the horsemen, killing or disorientating so many that they became prey for the samurai swords and spears. The firearms alone did not win the battle, which lasted for eight hours of bitter fighting, but Nagashino showed that victories could be won by a combination of samurai and ashigaru under firm leadership.

It is important to note that the word 'ashigaru' does not necessarily indicate that the man in question was formerly a peasant farmer. At the beginning of the Period of Warring States the status boundary between poor samurai and wealthy farmers was not clearly drawn, and there was something of a grey area in between covered by men called 'ji-samurai'. Most ji-samurai were part-time samurai and, out of necessity, part-time farmers, and their tiny fiefs were particularly at risk from the expansive tendencies of the

daimyô. This often forced the ji-samurai to make the decision as to whether to stay as farmers, or to become a daimyô's soldiers. Many chose the latter, changing their residences from the villages to the barracks of the growing castle towns, and most began their military careers as ashigaru.

A peasant farmer whose only military equipment is a sword and shinguards. He retains his sickle and carries a sharpened bamboo pole as a spear. Men like these became ashigaru in the daimyô armies.

Toyotomi Hideyoshi

The best example of an ashigaru working his way through the ranks is Toyotomi Hideyoshi (1536-98), the so-called 'Napoleon of Japan'. Hideyoshi's father was an ashigaru in the service of Oda Nobunaga's father Oda Nobuhide. During a battle he was shot in the leg and forced to withdraw from all combat duties. As a result he lost the relationship he had with the Oda family and returned to the fields. His son, by contrast, rose through the ranks as he gained the confidence of Oda Nobunaga. After Nobunaga's death Hideyoshi fought a series of brilliant campaigns and went on to rule the whole of Japan, but once he had achieved his goal Hideyoshi began to pull up behind him the ladder of promotion that he had scaled so successfully. In 1588, when his conquest of the country was almost complete, he ordered the 'Sword Hunt', a nationwide confiscation of all weapons from the peasantry. It was an audacious move that no national leader had ever attempted before, but such was Hideyoshi's power that it was largely successful.

Following the Sword Hunt, the supply of casual ashigaru for hire virtually dried up, forcing all the daimyô in Japan to rely on their own men to form their armies, and then in 1591, with all the daimyô now acknowledging his suzerainty, Hideyoshi produced a further edict that set this distinction in stone. It forbade any change in status from samurai to farmer, or from farmer to anything, whether merchant or ashigaru. As this edict is so important in understanding the evolution of the ashigaru I shall quote sections from it at length:

'If there should be living among you any men formerly in military service who have taken up the life of a peasant since the seventh month of last year, with the end of the campaign in the Mutsu region, you are hereby authorised to take them under surveillance and expel them . . .

Here a gang of casual ashigaru overpower a defeated samurai who has crawled away from a battlefield. They wear a typical mixture of looted armour, and they seem set to add one more suit to their collection. (E.G. Heath collection)

'If any peasant abandons his fields, either to . . . become a tradesman or labourer for hire, not only should he be punished but the entire village should be brought to justice with him . . .

'No military retainer who has left his master without permission shall be given employment by another . . .

'Whenever this regulation is violated and the offender allowed to go free, the heads of three men shall be offered in compensation . . .'

The ashigaru of the defeated daimyô were therefore forbidden to return to the soil, and the newly disarmed farmers were finally and legally cut off from following in Hideyoshi's own illustrious footsteps. From 1591 onwards, therefore, we have a vastly different situation from the one that existed before. A peasant called up for service would in future be only a labourer, and any ashigaru carrying a heavy bullet box on his back could think himself lucky that despite his lowly status, he had at least one foot on the rungs of the samurai ladder.

The process of implementing the Separation Edict was a long one, and was only completed by Hideyoshi's successor Tokugawa Ieyasu (1542-1616). The ashigaru were already recognised as the 'other ranks' of a Japanese army, without whom victory could not be gained. With the establishment of the Tokugawa hegemony there came a rigid separation of the social classes of Japanese society. At the top were the samurai, and the ashigaru were there among them, being from then on officially defined as the lowest ranks of the samurai class.

With this acknowledgement of the ashigaru as samurai came a further recognition in a remarkable and unique book produced by a leading commander of the time. This work, entitled *Zôhyô Monogatari*, which translates literally as 'The Soldier's Tale', was written in 1649 by a serving samurai who had command of ashigaru and wished to pass on to posterity his own tips on how to get the best out of them. The author was Matsudaira Nobuoki, the son of Matsudaira Nobutsuna who commanded the Shogun's forces during the Shimabara Rebellion of 1638, the last action in which samurai armies were to be engaged. As the Shimabara Rebellion was conducted by renegade Christian samurai and disaffected farmers, Matsudaira Nobuoki may have learned several lessons from observing the tenacity and fighting skills of his opponents. The real significance of *Zôhyô Monogatari* lies in the fact that it was written at all. The wars of the 12th century produced a literature that concentrated almost exclusively on the individual prowess of named samurai. *Zôhyô Monogatari* is a handbook for the commanders of ashigaru, a class of fighting man whom the writer of the *Heike Monogatari*, for example, preferred to regard almost as non-existent. By 1649 the ashigaru were recognised for the immense contribution they could make to samurai warfare.

A section from *Ehon Taikô ki* showing a group of disciplined ashigaru spearmen. The man at the front has a rising sun *mon* (badge) on the front of his armour. The others wear the typical lampshade-shaped iron *jingasa* (war hat). Their spear shafts are very long.

ASHIGARU RECRUITMENT

The history of the ashigaru is that of a move from a casual, poorly trained infantry arm towards a more professional organisation with continuity of service, and nowhere is this better illustrated than in the methods of recruitment.

The casual nature of ashigaru activity during the Ônin War (1467-77) ensured that the rate of desertion often matched the rate of enlistment, and on some occasions an army could be swelled by bands of opportunistic ashigaru without the commander actually knowing they were there. Such men prowled around the extremities of a campaign like vultures, and were practically indistinguishable from the ghoulish peasants who roamed battlefields by night, finishing off wounded samurai and stealing their possessions.

In addition to this uncertain way of recruiting, the daimyô also drew footsoldiers from the men who worked his own lands, whether they were peasants or ji-samurai. As the years went by, and such daimyô territories became more widespread, so the means of recruiting ashigaru became less haphazard and more systematic. The final stage in this evolution was the transformation of ashigaru into full-time soldiers.

Until about 1580 the pressure on resources ensured that most daimyô had to use their ashigaru in the dual roles of soldiers and farmers, and it was only when campaigns began to be of longer duration that problems arose with this system. It was then inevitable that the wealthier landowners who could spare men for fighting without affecting agricultural production, would develop both economically and militarily. Success also bred success, because a victorious daimyô would attract followers for both purposes, thus making it even easier to arrange a division of labour. Some of the increase in numbers came from the opportunistic ashigaru who a

BELOW **The final evolution of the ashigaru was to a uniformly dressed infantryman, as shown in this excellent illustration from *Zôhyô Monogatari*. Note how the ashigaru has thrust his two swords through his *uwa-obi* (belt) before putting his armour on. The two tube-like sleeves are tied at the front and rear. His long trousers are fastened in at the knee and the ankle. The two shoulder straps on the armour with their toggles, and the tying cords for the side, are clearly illustrated. His cloth tube of provisions is shown on the ground. Each tied section was a day's ration of rice.**

century before would have moved on after a battle and now chose to stay, while a few managed to leave an unsuccessful daimyô for a more promising master. In some cases there was a wholesale movement of allegiance when defeated enemies were absorbed into a victor's hegemony. Contrary to the popular view, samurai warfare rarely ended with mass acts of either slaughter or *hara-kiri* (ritual suicide by disembowelment with a sword). Defeated daimyô were often encouraged to surrender their territories, and with them their farmers and warriors, for the guarantee of being reinvested in their original holdings in exchange for a pledge of allegiance.

The call to arms

For most of the daimyô, therefore, the recruitment of ashigaru consisted simply of a call to arms among their part-time soldiery, tearing them away from their farms when danger threatened. The excitement of war, the very real prospect of promotion, and the break from the routine of agricultural work was an inviting prospect to many, and it was said of the followers of Chôsokabe Motochika (1539-99) that they were so ready for a fight that they tended the rice fields with their spears thrust into the earth of the

A rare depiction of an ashigaru in a woodblock print. The ashigaru is shown as a samurai's attendant. He wears the standard ashigaru jingasa.

pathways and had their straw sandals attached to them. These enthusiastic part-time samurai and ashigaru served the Chôsokabe well, enabling them to gain control of the whole of the island of Shikoku. In 1585, however, these brave volunteers were defeated by the overwhelming force of Toyotomi Hideyoshi's highly trained and modern army, which invaded Shikoku. The full-time military role of Hideyoshi's army, whose ashigaru did little, if any, agricultural work and whose samurai did none at all, was a development that most contemporary daimyô simply could not afford.

The successful response to a call to arms, which the Chôsokabe would expect, depended on much more than the allure of a break from farming duties, and had its basis in the feudal structure of Japanese society. A well-organised daimyô knew in minute detail the extent of the territory he owned, because registers of landholdings listed the lands granted to retainers, who held them in a system of mutual obligation. These men, who were of the samurai class, received lands from the daimyô, and in return were 'retained' in his service, hence the word 'retainer'.

The most important aspect of this retained service was, of course, to serve in the daimyô's army both in a personal capacity as a samurai and also to provide other troops in the lord's service. The number of troops supplied and their equipment depended upon the samurai's recorded wealth, which was expressed in terms of the assessed yield of the rice fields he possessed. Such assets were traditionally measured in 'koku', one koku being the amount of rice thought necessary to feed one man

LEFT **Standard ashigaru equipment: the jingasa, belt, okegawa-dô armour, ration bags and float for river crossings.**

An ashigaru jingasa, lacquered black and with a gold mon. (Courtesy of the Nagashino Castle Preservation Hall)

for one year. This is how the ashigaru entered the story. The samurai knew exactly how many men he was required to take with him on campaign. Some would be other samurai who were usually related to him. The rest would be ji-samurai or farmers who may not have had long family connections, but as the years went by and casual recruitment became less common, a family tradition of service to a particular samurai family would develop.

With promotion dependent almost entirely on performance, and performance being assessed in terms of the number of heads taken, the loyal and brave ashigaru could achieve at a personal level what Hideyoshi was to formalise in 1591 at a legal level, namely, the integration of the ashigaru into the samurai class as its lower ranks. The existing overlap between a poor landowning ji-samurai and a well-rewarded ashigaru, therefore, became increasingly blurred until Hideyoshi and Ieyasu abolished the distinction by making them both 'samurai'. To misquote Napoleon, 'every ashigaru carried a general's war fan in his knapsack'.

Yet while there was an overlap between the ashigaru and the samurai above them, until 1591 there was an additional overlap between the ashigaru who carried equipment for a daimyô and the huge numbers of people who could be virtually press-ganged into an army when extra labouring work was needed. Hideyoshi's Separation Edict ensured that the only active service peasants could now supply was as labourers, because weapon use was officially forbidden to them. Yet this was no drawback for a general, as the advances in military technology meant that, without training in group fighting with long spears and arquebuses, a peasant would be a liability in an army rather than an asset.

Prior to 1591, therefore, we see labouring and fighting duties being mixed up and allotted according to experience and need. An enhanced use of labourers and carriers is particularly apparent for campaigns of

This illustration is from a modern Japanese comic book by the accomplished manga artist Junko Miki, and it shows a group of ashigaru resting on a battlefield. Their long spears and cloth sunshades are well depicted.

long duration such as sieges, when considerable demands were made on the population in numbers required and in the range of services offered. For example, the Takeda family operated a number of gold mines, and the miners were ideal for tunnelling under an enemy's castle walls. A detailed muster list for similar non-combatant service is provided in the records of the Shimazu family of Satsuma in southern Kyushu. In 1576 the Shimazu attacked the fortress of Takabaru, and in their call to arms listed many labouring duties in addition to fighting.

A jingasa, made of lacquered papier-mâché, bearing the mon of the Tachibana.

Permanent units

At the other end of the ashigaru social scale were the elite ashigaru who were kept almost permanently 'under the colours', a state of affairs that was confined to a daimyô's personal bodyguard for much of the period under examination. A good example is provided by the Hôjô family. The Hôjô, who were based around the area of present-day Tokyo, prospered as successful daimyô over five generations until their castle of Odawara surrendered to Toyotomi Hideyoshi in 1590. A samurai called Okamoto Hachirôza'emon Masahide belonged to the Hôjô daimyô's *go-uma mawari-shû* (honourable horse guards) based at Odawara castle, and had to supply his own personal service with horse, plus four samurai (unmounted), six ashigaru spearmen, two ashigaru flag bearers, and two others who would act as reserves.

Both Okamoto and the ashigaru under his command were based permanently in Odawara castle. Not only is the weaponry of his followers recorded, but also their names, indicating the continuity of service that was later to become universal. The names of his men do, however, show one fundamental difference between samurai and ashigaru, because the four samurai have surnames, while the ashigaru have none. Any ashigaru who fought his way to samurai status soon took a surname, of which one of the written characters was often derived from the surname of his master or an admired ally. This neat illustration of class distinction reminds us that even though the ashigaru service was definitely valued, the samurai still regarded them as their social inferiors.

In contrast to Okamoto's contribution to a permanent unit, another retainer of the Hôjô called Ôtô Nagato no kami was called upon to supply a contingent of 252 men at the time of the Odawara campaign in 1590. The numbers were made up from 75 mounted samurai, 36 foot samurai, 115 ashigaru and 26 labourers. Most of these men would still be part-time farmers, showing how far behind the Hôjô were in military development compared to their rival Toyotomi Hideyoshi.

An earlier example of a Hôjô 'call to arms' is the document issued in about 1560 by Hôjô Ujimasa (1538-90), which shows how a farmer on standby could quickly become an ashigaru:

'1. All men, including those of the samurai class in this country district, are ordered to come and be registered on the 20th day of this month. They are to bring with them a gun, spear, or any kind of weapon, if they happen to possess one, without fearing to get into trouble.

2. If it is known afterwards that even one man in this district

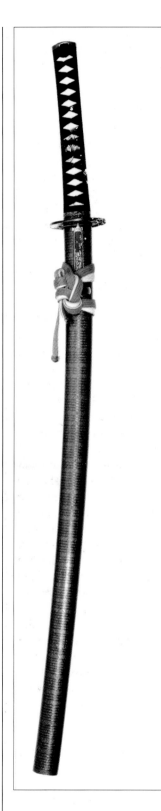

concealed himself and did not respond to the call, such man, no matter whether he is a commissioner or a peasant, is to be beheaded.

3. All men from 15 to 70 years of age are ordered to come; not even a monkey tamer will be let off.

4. Men to be permitted to remain in the village are those whose ages are above 70 years, or under 15 years, and too young to be used as messengers, but the others are all ordered to come.

5. It will be good for the men to prepare for the call by polishing their spears and preparing small paper flags to be taken with them. Those who are fitted to be messengers, and desire to do that service, will be so permitted.

6. All the men covered by this order are to come to Katsukui on the 4th day and register before the lord's deputy and then return home. If the appointed day happens to be rainy they are to come the first day the weather is settled. Men must arrive at the appointed place properly armed with anything they happen to possess, and those who do not possess a bow, a spear or any sort of regular weapon are to bring even hoes or sickles.

7. This regulation is generally applicable, and even Buddhist priests who desire to do their duty for their native province are ordered to come.

It is ordered to pay strict attention to the implications of the above seven articles, and if there be anyone who disregards this ordinance and neglects his duty, such a one is to be severely punished; while the man who is careful and eager to be loyal to his lord will be rewarded with the grant that is reasonable and suitable to him.'

Rapid response units

The invasion of one's province by an enemy did not allow the leisurely assembly described above. In such a situation the farmers not only needed to become ashigaru within hours rather than days, which implied considerable readiness and preparation on their part, but the clan itself needed an efficient internal communications system to enable the call to arms to be transmitted rapidly. The most successful daimyô to tackle this problem was Takeda Shingen (1521-1573), one of the greatest military leaders of his age, who established a series of fire beacons known as noroshi throughout his territories. The noroshi were elaborate devices mounted on a three-storey wooden tower. The watcher, who was probably an ashigaru, stationed himself on the upper platform, while the beacon itself consisted of an iron bucket mounted at the end of a long tree trunk pivoted in its centre from a bracket fastened to the upper storey. On spotting the signal from the next beacon along, the watcher would hurry down the ladders and set fire to the combustible materials already prepared in the bucket. By pulling on ropes the beacon bucket would be swung high into the air. The system allowed observers on the edges of the Takeda territories to communicate directly with Kôfu, the Takeda capital, by a series of beacon chains.

Fire beacons were supplemented by fast horses ridden by scouts who passed the call on to local runners. By such means, the population of the Takeda territories was transformed into a fighting machine, multiplying tenfold the small permanent garrisons of samurai and ashigaru, and the large, 3,000-plus unit that made up Takeda Shingen's personal

The *katana*, the weapon that was universal among all ranks in a samurai army.

bodyguard. In later years, of course, practically an entire daimyô's army would be permanently 'under the colours', but in the mid-16th century the basis of ashigaru use was the call to arms from part-time soldiers.

ORGANISATION AND COMMAND

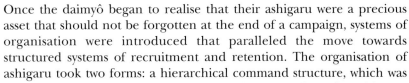

An illustration from the Meiji Period showing an ashigaru of the 1850s wearing a long coat in addition to his jingasa. His arquebus rests in a leather bucket, and he has a large cartridge box.

Once the daimyô began to realise that their ashigaru were a precious asset that should not be forgotten at the end of a campaign, systems of organisation were introduced that paralleled the move towards structured systems of recruitment and retention. The organisation of ashigaru took two forms: a hierarchical command structure, which was invariably headed by samurai, and a sideways specialisation of the three weapon groups of arquebus, bow and spear.

The overall command of the specialised ashigaru units was vested in respected and reliable samurai who were usually known as *ashigaru taishô*. Evidence that they were as highly regarded as commanders of purely samurai units is provided by the appearance of men bearing the rank of ashigaru taishô within the elite of the Takeda family who were known as the 'Twenty-four Generals'. Saigusa Moritomo, killed at the battle of Nagashino in 1575, was an ashigaru taishô, as was Hara Toratane who, it was said, could make ten ashigaru fight like 100 samurai.

The highest of the actual ashigaru ranks was the *ashigaru kashira* ('captain'). The ashigaru kashira would have command of an ashigaru company, which was more than likely to be homogeneous in terms of weapon function. The one exception to this was the inclusion of archers among the arquebus corps to keep up the fire during reloading, as illustrated by the *Kôyô Gunkan*, which notes a unit of 'ten arquebuses and five bows'.

Beneath the ashigaru-kashira were the *ashigaru ko gashira* ('lieutenants'). In the *Kôyô Gunkan* one ashigaru kashira has five ashigaru ko gashira serving under him to command his company of 75 archers and 75 arquebusiers, so that every ko gashira has responsibility for 30 men. The ashigaru ko gashira was a vital element in the chain of command because the ordinary ashigaru in their weapon squads served directly under him. The *Zôhyô Monogatari* notes how a ko gashira was selected:

'In the firearms squads they were chosen on the basis of marksmanship and speed of fire, the possession of a calm spirit, one who would not disengage when the enemy bullets began.'

Weapon specialisation

The sideways division of the ashigaru was by weapon speciality, between arquebus, bow and spear. In 1592 the Shimazu army that went to Korea included 1,500 archers, 1,500 arquebusiers and 300 spearmen, while in 1600 the Date family supplied the Tokugawa with 200 archers, 1,200 arquebusiers and 850 spearmen. One trend that can be readily identified is an overall increase in the number of firearms possessed, even if the proportion of them to other arms varies considerably. By 1530 missile weapons in the form of bows had already tended to become the province of the lower class warrior, leaving the samurai free to engage in spear fighting at close quarters with a worthy opponent. It was, therefore, only natural that the new missile weapon, which had an even greater range, should be similarly regarded. We read in the *Jôsen Kidan*:

'As a rule, on the battlefield, it is the job of the ashigaru to face on to the enemy and fire arquebuses in volleys into the midst of the enemy. As for the arquebuses owned by samurai, they are for shooting and bringing down an enemy of importance.'

The Korean campaign saw devastating use made of massed arquebuses, leading to one general writing home to argue that any soldiers who were sent to Korea should bring guns with them. No other weapon was needed.

The firearms squads were supplied with an arquebus that was based on the design introduced to Japan by the Portuguese in 1543. It was fired when a smouldering match fastened into a serpentine was dropped on to the touch hole, and unlike primitive hand guns the model had reached a sufficient degree of sophistication for this process to be operated from a sprung trigger. To prevent premature discharges, the touch hole was closed until the point of firing by a tight fitting brass cover. In 1549 the Shimazu clan of Satsuma became the first samurai to use arquebuses in battle.

One disadvantage of the arquebus was its slow loading time compared to the bow, making it necessary for archers to provide cover while reloading took place. The experience of the battle of Nagashino confirmed volley firing as the most effective way of using arquebuses, but it also illustrated the iron-hard discipline needed to make it work. Rain was of course an enormous problem, but it was one that affected friend and foe alike in a field battle, and fuses were weatherproofed by boiling them in various mixtures, such as tooth-blackening powder!

The arquebus men were under the direct command of a *teppô ko gashira* (lieutenant of the firearms squad). Judging by their representation on painted screens, a firearms unit would comprise a series of groups of gunners, at least five per group, with each group accompanied by an archer. A number of these groups (between one and

The *teppô ko gashira* were the lieutenants of the firearms squads. This man (from *Zôhyô Monogatari*) would have direct command of the arquebusiers. His badge of office is his red-lacquered 'swagger stick', which is a bamboo tube in which is concealed a sturdy ramrod. The swagger stick could be used by an arquebusier should his own ramrod break. The ko gashira also has a spare length of fuse wrapped round his left arm.

2

4

The members of an arquebus squad from *Zôhyô Monogatari*.
1. An ashigaru armed with his arquebus. He has placed a set of spare ramrods in a cloth in his belt like a quiver of arrows, lest one should break. His fuse is tied around his left wrist.
2. An ashigaru with his arquebus carried over his shoulder.
3. An ashigaru holding a ramrod. His arquebus is slung through his belt.
4. The arquebusiers could not pick up their enemies' missiles as could the archers, so bullet carriers, like this man who wears a heavy box on his back, kept the firearms squads supplied.

six) would be answerable to an individual ko gashira, but the exact number varied enormously from daimyô to daimyô. The ko gashira was recognisable by his possession of a length of red-lacquered bamboo reminiscent of a swagger stick, in which was kept a strong ramrod in case any gunner's ramrod broke during action.

Large numbers of ashigaru archers were also employed throughout the Period of Warring States. Some may have been highly trained sharp-shooters used as skirmishers or for sniping, but their most important role was to fire volleys of arrows. The bow was a longbow made from bamboo and rattan and lacquered for protection against damp. Even though they had a shorter range than the arquebus, and required a more practised operator, their rate of fire was more rapid and enemy arrows could be re-used. Archers were supported by carriers who were at hand with large quiver boxes containing 100 arrows. The preferred

range for firing was from between 30 and 80 metres, and the bow had a maximum effective range of 380 metres.

The training that both sets of missile troops required must have been quite extensive. Even though the training required for the simple operation of an arquebus looked far less than that required to produce a marksman archer with the necessary muscular strength to draw the bow, any 'training dividend' that this produced was countermanded, as in Europe, by the extra training that arquebusiers needed for speed in reloading and the discipline of firing rotating volleys.

Spearmen

The other specialised arm were the spearmen, who almost always outnumbered missile troops within an army. Oda Nobunaga, who was probably the first to introduce disciplined ashigaru spear units, possessed a contingent that made up 27 per cent of his fighting force, compared to 13.5 per cent for the arquebusiers. In 1575 the Uesugi had ten spearmen for every arquebusier, and by about 1570 the breakdown of weaponry within the Hôjô armies included between 33 per cent and 50 per cent of all men (samurai and ashigaru) armed with spears. Within the Takeda clan, the proportion was between 50 per cent and 66 per cent.

The earliest ashigaru spears had been the same length (about three or four metres) as samurai ones, and were wielded just as freely in the conflicts of the Ônin War. A noticeable lengthening of the shaft of the ashigaru weapon follows from about 1530, producing the *nagae-yari* (long-shafted spear) which was more akin to a pike. A call to arms issued by Hôjô Ujimasa in 1587 includes the words, 'They are to bring with them any of the following three weapons: a bow, a spear or a gun. However, a spear, whether its shaft is made of bamboo or wood, is useless if it is shorter than two ken [about four metres].' The increase in length came about

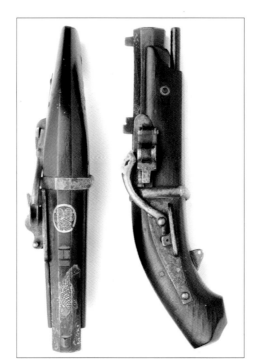

because a very different technique was developed for ashigaru spear fighting as distinct from samurai spear fighting. The samurai were regarded as individual spearmen who would engage in single combat with their weapons. The ashigaru spearmen were trained to fight as a group formed up in a line of two or three ranks with their spear points even, thus showing certain similarities to European pikemen.

The shaft of a nagae-yari was of composite construction, with a core of hardwood such as oak, surrounded by laminations of bamboo. Like the bows, the whole shaft was

This Japanese arquebus has an external brass spring. The trigger releases the serpentine, which drops the glowing match onto the touch hole. A brass cover protects the firing pan. The barrel is fitted with a backsight and a foresight. Note the short stock, the weapon would be hand-held rather than rested on the shoulder.

RIGHT Detail of the trigger and touch-hole mechanism of an arquebus, as shown on a miniature example.

lacquered to weatherproof it. The total length of nagae-yari differed from clan to clan according to the general's preference, the length of shaft was usually about three ken. At the start of the Period of Warring States one ken was equivalent to 1.6 metres (the dimensions changed later to 1.8 metres), so the length of the spear shaft would have been 4.8 metres. The Takeda used a nagae-yari shaft of three ken. Uesugi Kenshin used a shaft of two-and-a-half ken, while his successor, Kagekatsu (1555-1623), used three ken at about the time of Sekigahara, as did Toyotomi Hideyoshi. The Tokugawa also used a three-ken shaft.

Oda Nobunaga used the longest spears of all, with a giant three-and-a-half ken (5.6 metres) shaft. This would appear to be a development Nobunaga adopted quite early in his career, because there is a reference in the *Shinchôkoki* dated at April 1553 to '500 three-and-a-half ken long spears'. His father-in-law Saitô Dôsan expressed amazement at Nobunaga's long shafts, which meant the user required as much training as a gunner.

Serving a samurai

An army would also have several other ashigaru employed to carry the personal possessions of a samurai and to serve him like the genin of the Gempei Wars. For example, the *zori tori* (sandal bearer) carried a samurai's footwear, among other duties equivalent to an officer's batman. Spare footwear was important, because Japanese straw sandals do not last long, and a particular treatise on Japanese armour states, 'An

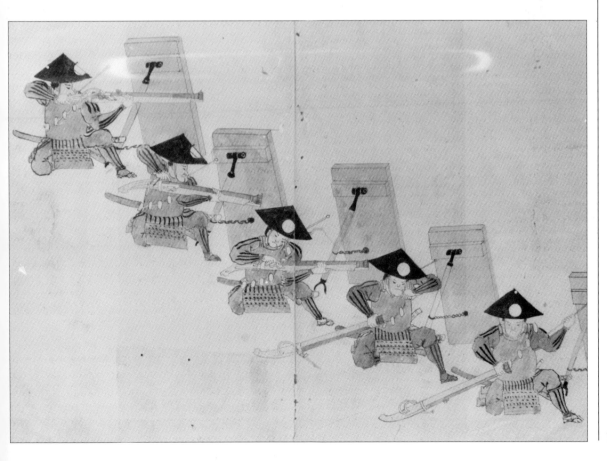

The *yumi ko gashira* (lieutenant of the archer squad) was the officer in charge, and one of his responsibilities, shown in this illustration from *Zôhyô Monogatari*, was to keep the archers supplied with arrows.

extra pair of sandals must be carried at your waist; this is quite as important a thing as carrying provisions.' Quite early in his career the great Toyotomi Hideyoshi, who had proved his worth as a fighting ashigaru, was promoted to the position of Oda Nobunaga's sandal bearer, and endeared himself to the latter by warming his master's sandals inside his shirt in cold weather.

A zori tori would also be found among that exclusive body of men who attended the daimyô himself. The greatest honour in this regard was attached to being the lord's *mochiyari gumi* (spear bearer). This man carried the samurai's personal polearm, and was a highly valued bodyguard, as the *Zôhyô Monogatari* tells us:

'As for the spear bearers, we invariably find them, and there is no place for cowards among their ranks, they serve with great devotion, and it is work of great merit. It is a tremendous thing to be used as a spear carrier, and a thing of ambition to serve the lord's needs.'

Other ashigaru carried his bow, his arquebus or his *naginata* (glaive), and many illustrations also show ashigaru carrying an assortment of spears with very elaborate scabbards. For example, Kimata Morikatsu, who was not himself a daimyô but merely a senior retainer of the Ii family of Hikone, was personally attended by the following men of ashigaru rank in 1600:

Personal ashigaru (including a sandal bearer)	4
Bearer of the cross-bladed spear	1
Bearer of the personal nobori (banner)	1
Groom	1

Kimata would also have had to supply samurai, each of whom was in turn served by a smaller group of attendants, plus a number of specialist ashigaru who would fight in the Ii weapon squads.

Signals and flag bearers

Other ashigaru would have the responsibility of operating the signalling devices used on a battlefield. The most commonly recorded is the *horagai* or shell trumpet. Drums were also used frequently. Smaller ones were carried on an ashigaru's back while a comrade beat the drum. Larger ones were suspended from a pole carried by two men, while the largest of all were mounted on a wooden framework, or built into a tower in a castle. Bells and gongs were also used. There was an agreed system of commands for advance or assembly, and armies marched to the beat of a drum.

The shift from a pattern of warfare between individuals to one of organised movements between groups is best illustrated by the large numbers of ashigaru who were employed in carrying flags. The vast majority would carry the long vertical *nobori* banners which were used to identify the locations of various units. Painted screens indicate that long rows of identical nobori would be found with each unit.

Members of the archery squads from *Zôhyô Monogatari*.
ABOVE **An ashigaru archer bends his bow against a support so that he can fit the string. He has a spare bowstring on a reel at his left side, and his quiver is covered with black bear fur.**
BELOW **The rapid fire of the ashigaru archers required a constant replenishment of arrows, so the arrow bearer carried a box with a load of 100 arrows on his back.**

The most prominent positions of all fell to the carriers of the *uma-jirushi* (literally 'horse insignia'). This was the device, often a flag, but sometimes a three-dimensional object, which acted as a samurai's standard and indicated his personal presence rather than that of a unit. A daimyô would possess an enormous *ô uma jirushi* (great standard), which was the nucleus of the army on the battlefield and attracted the heaviest fire. Smaller devices (including the *ko uma jirushi* or 'lesser standard') were carried in a leather bucket fastened to the ashigaru's belt, while large ones were strapped securely into a carrying frame worn on the back. Ropes were provided for the ashigaru standard bearer to steady his flag in a wind or on the run, and in the case of the large examples two comrades would hold two separate ropes to keep it steady.

Certain other ashigaru roles are not reflected in muster lists. For example, ashigaru would have the responsibility of operating the Takeda fire beacon chain, and a daimyô with his own navy, or one who acted as admiral, used ashigaru as sailors and marines. While some rowed the clumsy warships others fired arquebuses from portholes, launched firebombs and wielded grappling hooks. Throughout the Period of Warring States there is also a steady development of a specialised artillery arm. Exploding firebombs launched from catapults are recorded as early as 1468. Each catapult was fired by a team of 40 ashigaru pulling simultaneously on ropes to swing a lever arm. By 1615 such teams had been replaced by gun crews operating European culverins to bombard Ôsaka castle. Other functions of the ashigaru are best discussed under the heading of campaign life, which will be found in the section that follows.

CAMPAIGN LIFE OF THE ASHIGARU

The ashigaru assembled through the muster system are now ready to set off on campaign, and we may imagine them leaving the castle gates in an orderly procession, with arquebuses, bows and long spears carried tidily on their shoulders. But whereas the function of the specialised ashigaru units is self-evident from their titles, the role of certain other ashigaru only becomes apparent when examined in the context of campaign life. As an example of the additional retinue that a

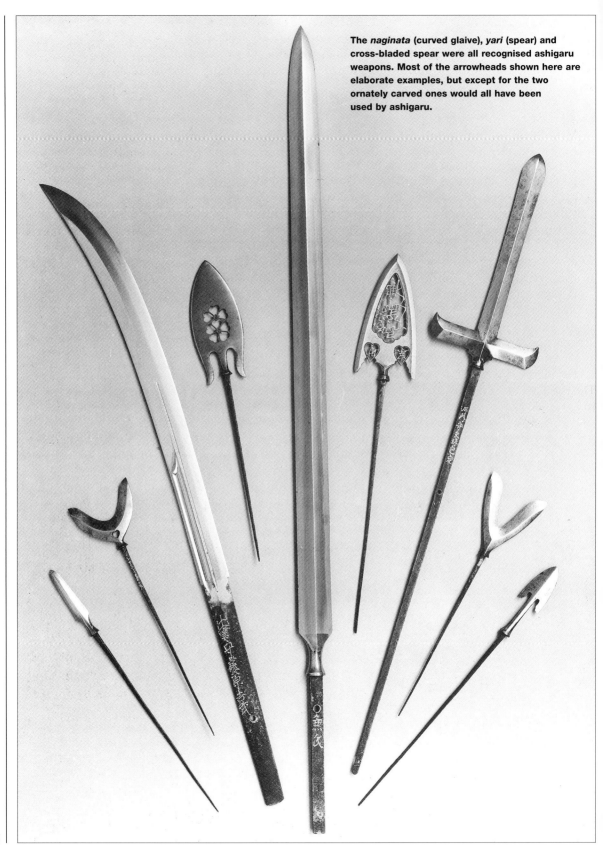

The *naginata* (curved glaive), *yari* (spear) and cross-bladed spear were all recognised ashigaru weapons. Most of the arrowheads shown here are elaborate examples, but except for the two ornately carved ones would all have been used by ashigaru.

high-ranking samurai might have been expected to have, the servants and general bearers who were in attendance on Kimata Morikatsu in 1600 are listed below, but it is important to make a distinction between ashigaru such as these and labourers who could be press-ganged into a daimyô's army.

Item	Number of men
Lantern carriers – 4 chests	4
Maku (field curtain) and standards in one large chest	2
Kitchen utensils – 2 chests	2
General porters – 2 packs	2
Food bearers – 2 packs	2
Packhorse leader	1
Fodder bearers – 3 packs	3
Grooms with spare horses	2
Gunpowder – one chest	1
Cloaks etc. for rainy conditions – 2 large chests	4
Bodyguard samurai armour – 2 large chests	4
Bodyguard ashigaru armour – one large chest	2
Another large armour chest	2
Kimata's own armour – one chest	1
Footwear bearer – one chest	1
Arquebuses and tools (bullet moulds etc.) – one large chest	2
Bullets, powder, arrows – one large chest	2

The large chests referred to were like small palanquins and were slung from a pole and carried by two men each, while a 'pack' is of bamboo

BELOW **The ashigaru spearmen were the third of the three specialised ashigaru units described in *Zôhyô Monogatari*. Two types of spears are found, the long *nagae-yari* (long-shafted spears) which were akin to European pikes, and the shorter *mochi-yari* (hand spears).**
LEFT **The mochi-yari is held by a *yari ko gashira* (spear corps lieutenant). Note how the spear blade is fitted with a scabbard, contrary to European practice.**
RIGHT **Two spearmen. The character on the viewer's right appears to have acquired three trophies of war: two swords, which he has tied on to the shaft of his mochi-yari, and the severed head of their former owner. Note how the cords of the skirts of the armour are draped over the scabbards of his own swords, thus allowing them to be drawn in *katana* style (blade uppermost) unlike the samurai practice of slinging them *tachi* style, with the blade downwards, from a sword hanger.**

and straw. Bales of rice were also carried on men's backs, on pack horses, or on two-wheeled carts pushed and pulled by bearers. Larger carts, pulled by oxen, were also used, and were particularly handy for transporting heavy cannon. European cannon were usually supplied only as barrels, and without a carriage.

Discipline was the key to a successful march. When Tokugawa Ieyasu advanced on Odawara in 1590 he issued a number of strict regulations concerning keeping order in ranks and the avoidance of disruption to the civilian population. There was to be no looting. This may seem a very noble sentiment, but they were his own territories through which his army was marching! Weapons also had to be carried according to set rules and horses had to be controlled.

When going on campaign, food supplies for men and horses were of paramount importance, as made clear by the *Zôhyô Monogatari*:

'Normally take food for ten days but no more. If continuing on a road for ten days distance, use pack horses, and do not leave them behind . . . As for the horse's food, store it safely in a bag when raiding enemy territory, do not abandon anything, and if suffering from hunger in a camp eat the vegetation. The horse can stick to dead leaves. It will also eat refined pine bark . . . As for firewood 80 monme is sufficient for one person for one day, and all can gather it together. If the place has no firewood take dried horse dung and use it as firewood.

'As for rice, for one person allow six go, and one go of salt for ten people, for miso [paste made from soya beans] allow for ten people two go, but when there is a night battle and so on the amount of rice should be increased.'

Horses

Horses could be particularly trying. 'When taking horses on a raid', says the *Zôhyô Monogatari*, 'you must be very careful. Young horses may break free and will get excited. Because of this an army could be defeated, so this must be strictly forbidden. Keep them well tied up to avoid this.' The other rigours of campaign life provided many challenges, of which the treatment of wounds was an important issue. The most gruesome account in the *Zôhyô Monogatari* concerns the methods for extracting arrowheads:

'Tie the hair up in a bag and use chopsticks to pull the arrow out. If it is not possible to pull the arrow shaft out using the hands, pincers may be employed. With these it should be possible.'

For removing an arrow stuck through the cheek the method is a little more stringent:

'The head must not move, so fasten him [the casualty] to a tree, and with the head tied to a tree like a crucifixion the work can begin.

This ashigaru from *Zôhyô Monogatari* is a *zori tori* (sandal bearer), the personal attendant on a daimyô or a very high ranking samurai.

A box for carrying a samurai's armour, which an ashigaru would have carried on his back.

The arrow can be pulled out gently, but while doing this the eye socket will be filled with blood.'

The most dramatic advice in the *Zôhyô Monogatari* concerns the treatment for snake bite in a bivouac:

'When lying down in a camp in a field or on a mountain, if an adder bites don't get over excited, speedily apply one monme of gunpowder to the spot. Set fire to it and the virulence will quickly disappear, but if it is delayed it will not work.'

Looting

When not fighting on a battlefield or marching to war, the enduring image of the common soldier in all cultures contemporary with the ashigaru is that he was the agent of pillage, destruction, arson and other havoc. We noted earlier that the origin of the ashigaru at the beginning of the Period of Warring States were the ne'er-do-wells who joined the armies for the prospect of loot. Now that ashigaru were integrated fully into the samurai army, did such activities continue on an official basis as an instrument of war?

Looting was sometimes necessary if a campaign proved to be of long duration in an enemy territory, and it was then usually regarded as fair game. The wise counsels of the *Zôhyô Monogatari*, however, took the view that looting could be avoided if the army was properly prepared:

'Nowadays 45 days allowance can be taken, but no more than three or four days should be forced on to a horse, but whether in enemy territory or that of allies there should be no unpreparedness. In such cases take food with you or you will have to seize food from allies, which would be foolish and also theft.'

These are sentiments which tally with Tokugawa Ieyasu's orders before Odawara, but if looting could not be avoided, then it may as well be successful, as the *Zôhyô Monogatari* says:

'Food and clothing may be buried inside houses, but if it is buried outside it may be concealed in a pot or kettle. When such things are buried in the ground, visit during an early morning frost, and at the places where things are buried the frost will disappear, and many things may be discovered.'

However, the ashigaru foragers are warned to be careful of booby traps left by an enemy:

'Remember that a dead person's blood may have contaminated the water supply you drink. You should never drink the water from wells in enemy territory. It may be that faeces have been sunk to the bottom. Drink river water instead. When provinces are exchanged take care with the water. In camp it is a good idea to drink water which has been in a pot with apricot kernels in silk, or put into the pot some freshwater snails brought from your own province and dried in the shade, and that water supply will be good to drink.'

The support functions of ashigaru are illustrated in this picture of the followers of Hôjô Sôun. One holds a flag, while others unload equipment and weapons from a boat.

Oda Nobunaga is attended by ashigaru spearmen who are wearing *okegawa-dô* (smooth-surfaced breastplates) with the *kusazuri* (skirts) tied up so as not to impede their progress in wooded countryside, from *Ehon Toyotomi Gunki*.

A samurai attended by ashigaru arquebusiers, a groom, a standard bearer and a baggage carrier, from *Ehon Toyotomi Gunki*.

In many cultures, of course, foraging and looting go hand in hand with acts of unnecessary cruelty to the civilian population, and in one very important aspect the Japanese situation was different from that in Europe. Nearly all its wars were civil wars, so an oppressed peasant could theoretically cross a provincial border to till the fields of an enemy, making cruelty against civilians most inadvisable. In support of this benevolent view it must be admitted that the most dramatic example of a peasant uprising against a cruel daimyô occurred two decades after the civil wars had ceased. This was the Shimabara Rebellion of 1637 to 1638, directed against the tyrant Matsukura Shigemasa, who was given to tying peasants inside straw raincoats and setting fire to them. From this it may be argued that if Matsukura had lived at a time when one's neighbour was by definition one's rival, then self-interest alone would have prevented him from acting in such an outrageous manner.

Civilian casualties

It is difficult to tease out much evidence of deliberate civilian casualties from contemporary Japanese writings, although it may simply be that the compilers did not think that such matters were worth recording. When Takeda Shingen was repulsed before Odawara castle in 1569 he burned the town of Odawara before retiring, but when Toyotomi Hideyoshi took Kagoshima in 1587 and Odawara in 1590 there was nothing that remotely resembled the sack of a European town. By contrast, civilian deaths are certainly implied in the accounts of wars conducted against peasant armies, such as Nobunaga's campaign against the Ikkô sectarians or the Shimabara Rebellion, where the distinction between soldier and non-combatant was blurred and the rebels took shelter in fortresses along with their families. Nobunaga took Nagashima in 1573 by building a palisade round it and burning the entire complex. The Shimabara Rebellion ended with a massacre, but, as noted above, the situation was by no means typical.

However, the Korean campaign of 1592-98 added a different dimension. Here there was no prospect of an ill-treated peasant joining the Japanese army (although some Korean renegades managed to benefit from the situation). The Japanese troops took what they wanted from Korean fields and towns as an act of war to supply their own needs, so we must undoubtedly accept a role for the ashigaru in pillage and plunder. As for unnecessary violence to civilians, there was one other important difference from the Japanese theatre of war. In Korea the fortified town often replaced the isolated castle as a battle site, and many civilian deaths must be inferred from the huge number of heads taken at such conflicts as Chinju and Namwôn.

The most powerful evidence of Japanese atrocities in Korea comes in the form of a unique and little-known document, the diary of a Japanese Buddhist monk called Keinen, who accompanied the daimyô Ôta Kazuyoshi as his personal chaplain and physician. Keinen secretly recorded his observations and feelings about the human suffering inflicted on the Korean population. His entries covering the fall of Namwon castle in 1597 include a chilling description of mass slaughter. Keinen reveals that the notorious (and incorrectly named) Ear Mound in Kyoto contains the noses not only of dead soldiers but also of

A daimyô sits surrounded by his bodyguard, among whom are many ashigaru wearing their characteristic jingasa, from a painted scroll in the Watanabe Museum, Tottori.

A fibreglass ashigaru armed with a spear mans the wooden walls of a Sengoku castle, as shown in this full-sized reproduction fort which forms the entrance to the Ise Sengoku Jidai Mura.

Neither of the two grooms shown in this illustration from *Zōhyō Monogatari*. wears any armour except for the jingasa helmet. The figure on the left has a wooden drinking cup thrust through the belt of his jacket. The groom on the right holds on to the horse. He has a spare bit and bridle slung around his neck, and has a whip in his belt. The details of the horse's saddle are well illustrated. The knot on the pommel is the place where the saddle girth was tied.

thousands of non-combatants: men, women and children. He also reveals that many hundreds more people were sent as slaves to Japan.

Another revealing point from Keinen's diary covers the cruel treatment that the samurai meted out to their own people. In this case, the victims were the Japanese labourers press-ganged into the invading army to complete the building of Ulsan castle:

'There are beatings for the slightest mistake in performing such tasks as tying knots. In many cases I have witnessed this becomes the last occasion on which the person gets into trouble ... Hell cannot be in any other place except here.'

In another section Keinen describes how a group of labourers were sent into the forests to cut timber and had to stay behind to trim the tree trunks. They were caught by a Chinese patrol and beheaded. He also describes labourers 'brought from thousands of miles away' bent double under the weight of the goods they were unloading at the ports for the Japanese war effort.

Apart from the shock of reading of such cruelty, Keinen's diary provides a remarkable illustration of the consequences of Hideyoshi's Separation Edict of 1591. There is now a complete distinction between the armed and uniformed ashigaru and the unarmed and despised peasant labourer. One need only consider that Toyotomi Hideyoshi, who masterminded the invasion, had begun life as a peasant, to appreciate how impossible such a rise through the ranks would now be for a member of this wretched press gang. It is therefore not surprising to hear of some peasant labourers concluding that they would be better off with the Koreans than their fellow Japanese, and absconding from the fortified camps. This is confirmed in the diaries of Admiral Yi Sun-sin, who interrogated some Japanese peasants captured by Korean soldiers. The diaries reveal that the peasants had been taken along into the army by the Shimazu family and had run away because of their ill treatment.

But why were they treated so cruelly? The samurai, after all, were expecting to return home and would then need these men to till their fields. Perhaps the answer lies in the immense and over-reaching single-mindedness of Toyotomi Hideyoshi which permeates the whole of the brutal Korean campaign. No one and nothing was spared in the achievement of his megalomaniac aims. There was no mercy shown either to Koreans, Chinese or Japanese caught up in this monstrous roller coaster of terror. Hideyoshi died while the war was still continuing, and within days of his death the armies were recalled. The daimyô who had fought in Korea then had either to suppress the truth about what happened or handle any discontent that arose, and it is perhaps significant that almost all the Korean veterans were to end up on the losing side in the battle of Sekigahara in 1600.

Field remedies

Yet whether a man was a samurai, an ashigaru or a labourer, anyone could be laid low by the rigours of a long campaign or a terrible siege. The *Zôhyô Monogatari* offered the following, somewhat naïve, advice for conditions where a padded haori jacket or a peasant's straw raincloak was insufficient to keep the cold at bay:

To be a weapon bearer to the daimyô was a tremendous responsibility. In this illustration from *Zôhyô Monogatari* we see the bearer of the lord's bow and arrows. The weapon and its missiles are fixed into a sturdy wooden frame, which could be positioned on a flat surface on its own.

'Concerning pepper grains, in both summer or winter take one each in the mornings, this will ward off the cold and encourage warmth. This can be varied by taking *umeboshi* [pickled plums]. If you apply squashed red peppers from the hips to the tips of the toes you will not freeze. It is also good to daub it on your arms too, but avoid the eyes and the eyeballs.'

Yet some conditions went far beyond a remedy from eating pepper grains. The bitter cold of the Korean winter deprived men of hands and feet from frostbite, and an eye witness of the siege of Ulsan in the bitter winter of 1597-98 noted how death from hypothermia made no distinction between samurai, ashigaru or labourer:

'29th day, and both friend and foe are silent. Nevertheless inside the castle we have maintained our defences by day and night without any sleep. Here and there inside the castle, at the sunny places on the walkways and at the foot of towers, without differentiating between samurai, ashigaru or labourers, 50 or 30 men at a time are bowed under the unbearable hunger, thirst and cold. Also, besides this, there are a number of men who let their heads drop and lie down to sleep. The soldiers take their spears and patrol, but it is a fact that there are some men who have not moved all day, and when they try to rouse them with the butt end of a spear, the ones who are completely bent over have been frozen to death.'

This illustration from *Geijutsu Hiden Zue* shows an ashigaru groom in attendance on a mounted samurai. The difference between the armour worn by the two men is marked.

THE ASHIGARU'S EXPERIENCE OF BATTLE

The ashigaru had a vital role to play on the battlefield, and this topic will now be examined from two directions: the theoretical and the practical. The theory involves such materials as modern experiments on firearm effectiveness plus Matsudaira's recommendations in the *Zôhyô Monogatari*, which, although written in 1649, was based on first-hand experience of ashigaru warfare. The practical sections identify accounts of ashigaru warfare from the chronicles and diaries of the period. These accounts are quite rare, and often we have to tease out the ashigaru involvement from the context, such as the use of firearms or the controlled use of spears.

One of the most important areas of military theory in 16th-century Japan was the existence of numerous models of battlefield layout. Most were based on old Chinese models, but all had certain features in common: the general to the rear centre, surrounded by his bodyguard; the cavalry units ready to charge; a vanguard of brave samurai and ashigaru missile troops protected by ashigaru spearmen; and a sizeable flank and rear contingent. The baggage train would be guarded to the rear. Different units would communicate with one another through the highly mobile *tsukai-ban*, the elite mounted samurai who acted as messengers. Other messengers would operate between allied contingents, who occupied different positions on the field.

The presence of allied contingents, and the definition of what constitutes an 'ally' rather than a subordinate commander, begs an important question with regard to ashigaru warfare. If two or more allied armies were present on a battlefield, did they combine their ashigaru weapons troops into, say, one large arquebus unit, or did they continue to operate separately?

In answering this question we must first appreciate the difference between a typical Japanese battle formation and the contemporary European pike and shot 'squares'. For example, at the battle of Fornovo in 1495 the Swiss packed 3,000 men into a 60 metre square. Nowhere do Japanese records imply such formations. The impression is always given of a much looser structure from which defence could quickly convert into lively offence. The way in which a Swiss pike square could make its steady and crushing advance while keeping formation also bears little resemblance to a Japanese army's 'charge', 'charge' being one of the most frequently used words in battle descriptions.

Within a particular daimyô's army a pooling of weaponry certainly took place. The examples noted earlier of Okamoto in the Hôjô army and Kimata in the Ii army indicate the men they were required to provide, not the men they were required to use. Both samurai would have retained the service of their personal attendants, but the

In one of the most interesting illustrations from *Zôhyô Monogatari* an ashigaru offers water to a horse, using his jingasa as a bowl. The horse, which is clearly troublesome, is tethered by a rope, and also has a band tied around its front legs. At the rear of the saddle are two bags containing rice and soy beans. The lord's matchlock pistol is in a holster at the right front of the saddle.

The most vulnerable men in an army were the ashigaru who carried flags. The ashigaru on the left has a *hata-jirushi* (flag streamer, fixed to a cross piece) which he carries in a leather bucket at his right side. Bravest of the brave were the men who carried the daimyo's *o uma jirushi*, which denoted the presence of the lord and attracted the fiercest fighting. The ashigaru on the right shows the large socket on the back of his armour into which the pole of the uma jirushi was slotted. It was secured by ropes.

arquebusiers and spearmen included in their muster requirements would serve in the specialist ashigaru squads. At the time of the Gempei Wars in the 12th century, however, the equivalent to Kimata would have had personal leadership of his own band of horsemen and footsoldiers in a very loose military structure. In the Warring States Period such command was subordinated to the greater good of the daimyô's army through a more systematic arrangement based on group fighting and weapon specialisation.

It is also apparent that the greater the social homogeneity in a daimyô's army, then the more precise and ordered were its tactics. Thus the fourth battle of Kawanakajima in 1561 involved very complex manoeuvring by night, but both armies were either Takeda men or Uesugi men, all of whom knew each other and had trained and served together. At Nagashino, Oda Nobunaga set up a very precise linear formation from troops who were either his vassals or those of one other allied army, the Tokugawa. The 3,000 arquebusiers selected for the volley firing were drawn from troops who fitted into an existing rank and social structure. The best example is the Shimazu, whose total social homogeneity allowed them to perfect the very difficult tactic of a false retreat.

The opposite situation, that of a coalition of allies, is seen to best effect at Sekigahara. Here Ishida Mitsunari commanded some very doubtful contingents, and the fact that Kobayakawa Hideaki was able to order his entire army to turn against their erstwhile comrades is proof that there was no pooling of weapon types across the whole command. However, there seems to have been little 'sharing' on the other side either, as we read of an advance by the 'Ii contingent', who were among Tokugawa Ieyasu's closest retainers, and would surely have been more than willing to pool their ashigaru along with others. In some cases we

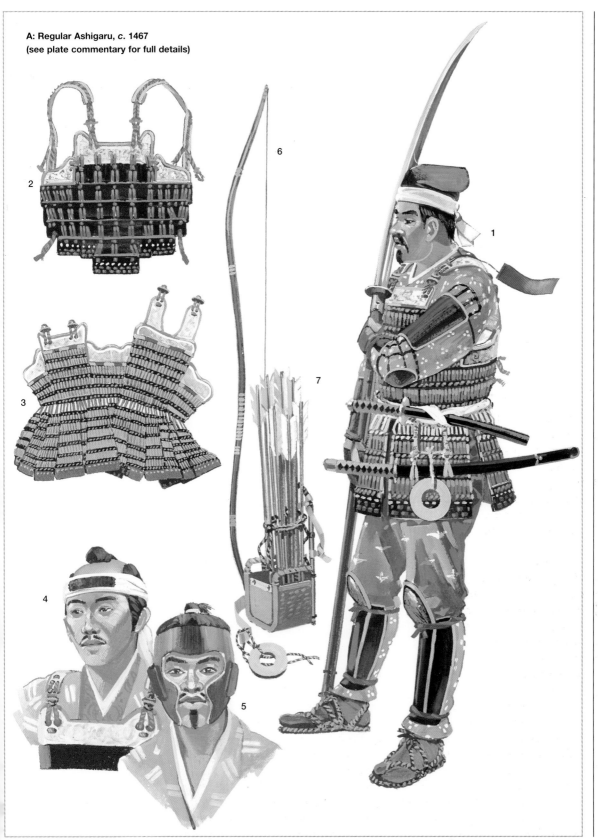

A: Regular Ashigaru, *c.* 1467
(see plate commentary for full details)

2

6

1

3

7

4

5

A

B: An Ashigaru spearman, c. 1592
(see plate commentary for full details)

B

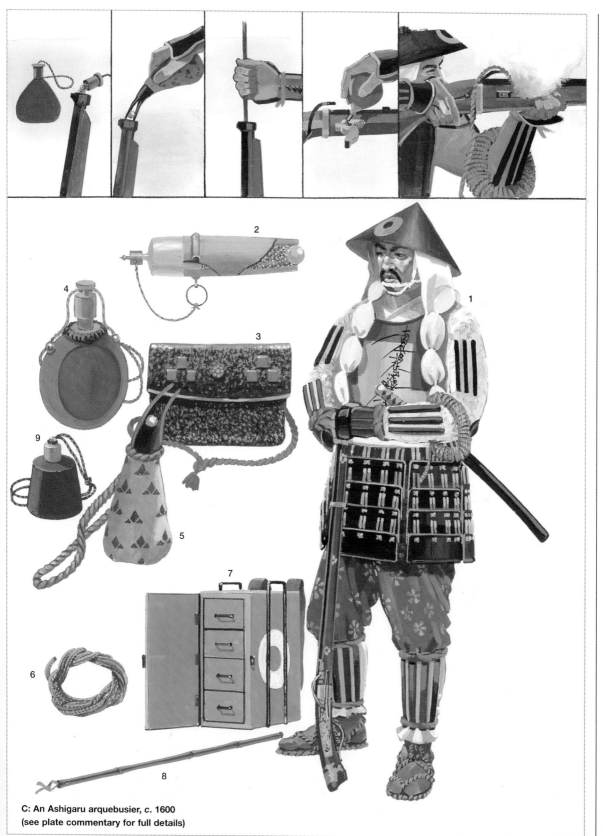

C: An Ashigaru arquebusier, c. 1600
(see plate commentary for full details)

C

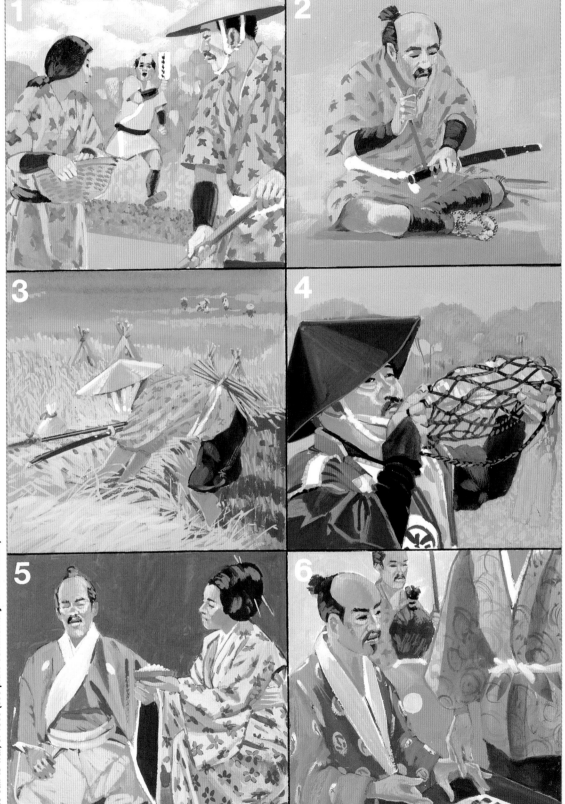

D: The call to war, c. 1560 (see plate commentary for full details)

E: Ashigaru training, c. 1550 (see plate commentary for full details)

F: Campaign life, northern Japan, 1591 (see plate commentary for full details)

F

G: Campaign life during the Shimabara rebellion, 1638 (see plate commentary for full details)

H: Ashigaru looting during the Onin War, 1467 (see plate commentary for full details)

H

I: Ashigaru operating catapult artillery, 1468 (see plate commentary for full details)

J: Ashigaru spearmen clash at Odawara, 1590
(see plate commentary for full details)

J

may also envisage different contingents, whether allies or subordinates, drawn up in very similar formations side by side, with only the change in the design on the flags being displayed indicating that this was not one complete army but several joined together.

The deployment of allies or subordinates as separate armies was occasioned by the vast scale of engagements like Sekigahara. The advantage was that different contingents could cover a wide area of possible activity. The disadvantage, however, was that weapon effectiveness was reduced, and that some contingents could change sides when they saw how the battle was going. The notorious Tsutsui Junkei, who fought at Yamazaki in 1582, only decided that he was for Hideyoshi when he saw the tide of battle going Hideyoshi's way. Up to that point he had simply watched and waited on a well-positioned hill.

Arquebus troops

Whatever the layout adopted, the growing importance of firearms meant that the first exchange of fire in a battle would probably be between the rival arquebus troops firing at a maximum range of about 100 metres. The firing would be controlled by the teppô kashira who commanded through the teppô ko gashira. Like the spearmen and archers they would be under the overall command of the samurai who bore the rank of ashigaru taishô. He would usually be stationed in the most forward position of all the samurai officers, and would thus be in the best position to judge when the firing had disorientated the enemy sufficiently for a charge to be ordered. At the ideal moment, the ashigaru spearmen advanced, and the samurai attacked vigorously on foot or horseback. While this was going on the ashigaru missile troops reorganised themselves under the protection of other ashigaru spearmen. In some situations the ashigaru archers supplied a volley of their own while the arquebusiers reloaded.

The response to arquebus fire varied enormously. Controlled volleys like those used at Muraki in 1554 and Marune in 1560 showed their effectiveness against a fortified position. The experience of the Takeda at Nagashino, who were almost broken by it, was an object lesson about the use of the arquebus from a fortified field position that was not wasted on other daimyô. Sometimes such volleys produced unexpected results, as when the poorly

One ashigaru blows a conch trumpet while another beats the war drum.

disciplined *rônin* (samurai who had lost their masters and joined other armies) of Osaka castle were goaded into action by gunfire at the battle of Tennôji in 1615.

In a recent practical assessment of an arquebus's range, five bullets were fired at a target in the shape of an armoured samurai from distances of 30 metres and 50 metres respectively. At 30 metres each of the five bullets hit the target area of the chest, but only one out of the five struck the chest when the target was moved back to 50 metres. Even at 50 metres, however, a bullet that struck home could do considerable damage, as shown by the results of a further experiment where a bullet pierced a 1mm iron plate at 50 metres. The scales of a typical lacquered *dô-maru* were of similar thickness.

A third experiment showed that an experienced Japanese arquebus enthusiast could perform the sequence of load, prime, aim and fire in as little as 15 seconds, a speed comparable to that of a flintlock musket. Other studies of arquebuses have shown that the need to keep the smouldering match out of the way while the pan is primed slows the process down to a more realistic rate of between 20 and 30 seconds, or in clumsy and inexperienced hands no better than one shot every minute. As we know that Nobunaga selected his 'best shots' for the line at Nagashino the rate of fire was probably quite high.

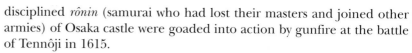

A small ivory statuette depicting an ashigaru blowing a *horagai* (conch shell trumpet), which was the main portable signalling device used in an army. The only point of detail that is not authentic is his rather expensive looking trousers.

Modern European experiments have revealed that operating an arquebus is a hazardous business. The force of the explosion has been found to dislodge the match, a problem the Japanese solved by inserting a tiny bamboo peg through holes in the serpentine. This would not, however, greatly add to safety, because the only sure way of preventing premature discharge was to remove the burning fuse completely away from the weapon.

The recommendations for successful ashigaru warfare in the *Zôhyô Monogatari* are arranged according to weapon group. Beginning with the arquebus, we see that there was great responsibility placed upon the shoulders of the ko gashira. His first duty was to distribute the bullets, which were carried in the bullet box by an ashigaru and then transferred to the bullet pouch worn at the gunners' belts. The leather bag in which the arquebus was carried was then carefully put to one side. When the enemy began to appear the fuse was inserted into the serpentine. If it was dropped in quickly or fitted badly the fire might go out, so a number of spare lighted fuses were kept on a metal stand thrust into the ground. Sound ramrods were another absolute necessity for the arquebusier:

'Use a ramrod that is made from oak, but even these will sometimes break. Without a ramrod the gunpowder cannot be forced down, so in most cases one man will have two or three, but the ko gashira carries a case in which a particularly sturdy ramrod is kept, and when there is difficulty getting the bullets in one can use it.'

Illustrations show spare ramrods being thrust through an ashigaru's belt. Ramming itself could be hazardous to one's comrades:

'When ramming do it up and down as far as the brim of the *jingasa*. If it is done out to one side there is a danger to the eyes of one's comrades, because other people's ramrods may be stuck in eyes, so it is best to lift it straight up and down.'

There was also the factor of the fouling of a barrel after a number of shots had been fired. In the case of an 18th-century

French flintlock, for example, fouling reduced the firing rate from one shot every 12 seconds to one shot every 45 seconds. Arquebuses were no different, and this is noted in the *Zôhyô Monogatari*, which states that: 'When five or six arquebus bullets have been fired there will be scorching inside the barrel and there will be difficulties with bullets getting stuck or with loading.'

The order to fire would be given when the enemy came within sufficient range. Nagashino provides the best example, as the precise locations of both the Takeda cavalry and the Oda arquebusiers are known. The arquebuses used at Nagashino had a maximum range of 500m, a distance at which even volley firing could be expected to do little damage. The maximum effective range for causing casualties was 200m, which was just a little less than the distance from the fence to the woods out of which the Takeda cavalry began their charge. It is highly unlikely that Nobunaga would have allowed any firing at this range, because the slight wounds caused would not have interrupted the flow of the charge and would have wasted at least one of the volleys. At 50m, which was approximately the distance from the fence to the little river called the Rengogawa that provided Nobunaga's outer line of defence, the effects would be more pronounced. Writing with the benefit of experience, the author of the *Zôhyô Monogatari* in 1649 recommends:

'As for the enemy, after beginning with the horses it is good to attack

This illustration from *Zôhyô Monogatari* shows an ashigaru wearing no armour except for a jingasa. He is likely to have been in charge of a pack-horse unit. He has two swords of simple design, as shown by the single coil of braid on the hilt. His provision bags are tied around his body.

The main means of transporting bulky loads on campaign was by packhorse battery. This illustration from *Zôhyô Monogatari* shows a packhorse, with two rice bales on its back. The horse also carries a small flag as an identification of the unit.

the riders. On these occasions fire at those riding the horses so that they fall off and also at the horses. It will disturb many of the enemy.'

In spite of all the noise, confusion and danger, an arquebusier would have had to give his total concentration to the business of reloading, ensuring that the touch hole was clear, that the bullet was correctly rammed down, and that there was no chance of the smouldering match causing a premature discharge.

At Nagashino the presence of the fence and the spearmen ashigaru, with their 5.6m long spears, would have provided the protection that the arquebusiers needed, and it is probable that any such combats at this time in the battle only occurred against Takeda cavalrymen who had passed through the gaps in the fence. This allowed the creation of a 'killing-ground' for separated horsemen, who became the prey both for samurai swords and ashigaru spears. To add to the defence from palisade and spear, dense clouds of smoke would also have been expected, a factor that this writer saw illustrated dramatically when observing arquebuses being fired at Nagashino in the annual festival.

Hand to hand fighting

The *Zôhyô Monogatari* also recognised that once the enemy had reached one's line, an unloaded arquebus is useless, so the author thoughtfully includes advice on when and how the arquebusiers themselves should engage in hand to hand fighting under the protection of the spearmen:

'If the enemy come close, because you will be replaced by men with spears, divide up to right and left. Remove the ramrod, sheathe the arquebus in the arquebus bag, and cross swords with them. Aim at the helmet, but if because the loan swords have dull blades you can only chop, aim at the enemy's hands and legs and you can cut at them.

'If the enemy are a distance away you can swab out the barrel, which is equivalent to cleaning it. At such time it is wise not to put powder and ball into the arquebus for about half a minute. While the enemy are out of sight carry the arquebus on your shoulder.'

One of the longest and most useful accounts of ashigaru on the battlefield is a passage in the chronicles of the Kuroda family describing the battle of Kimhae in 1592. It contains an excellent description of the deployment of arquebusiers and confirms the reliance placed on such men. The background is as follows. The first two divisions of the Japanese army of invasion landed in Korea at the port of Pusan. The third division was under the command of Kuroda Nagamasa, who was loathe simply to disembark in a port now occupied by Japan. Accordingly he sailed to the west to land at Kimhae, where there was more prospect of samurai glory.

The weapon that was less used in the Warring States Period than on previous occasions was the *naginata* (glaive). This ashigaru is the guard of the pack battery in an illustration from *Zôhyô Monogatari*.

'. . . the overall commanders of the vanguard ashigaru, Yoshida Nagatori and Uehara Shinza'emon went as the vanguard for the entire army and captured the boats at the shore side, then having seen that all was well from on board, half the ashigaru landed, led by the kashira. This first unit quickly ran up to a low piece of raised ground, and when they saw that they had taken up a position with their arquebuses, the remaining ashigaru under Nagatori and Shinza'emon also disembarked.

'They [the commanders] landed the horses and mounted them, and galloped off to nearby high ground, while in addition positions were taken with arquebuses among the bamboo and wooded areas. After this the five ranks of the whole army successively disembarked without difficulty. Subsequently the 100 arquebus ashigaru divided into two. The advance unit reformed their original ranks and turned against the enemy, and attacked the left flank of the enemy who were withdrawing from the second unit, firing arquebuses. Seeing the signs that the Korean soldiers were shaken by this, those who remained advanced as one, and many arquebuses were fired. Because the enemy were arranged in close ranks no bullets were wasted, and they fell in rapid succession. Nagamasa saw this and ordered the conch to be blown, brandished his *saihai* [baton of command] and gave the signal to advance.'

An account which is much briefer, but very useful because it quantifies the effects of arquebus fire, is found in the *Kirin Gunki*:

'There was a dreadful noise in the castle as over 100 shooters attacked, accompanied by about 60 horsemen. The arquebuses of the

One of the great drawbacks of the arquebus was its inability to fire in wet weather. Several ideas were tried to overcome this difficulty, such as weather-proofing the fuse by boiling it in a chemical mixture. One later innovation is shown here in a picture from *Geijutsu Hiden Zue*. A small box is fitted over the touch hole, allowing the whole operation of firing to take place under cover.

In this section from *Ehon Toyotomi Gunki* ashigaru are carrying straw bales packed with rice. The operation is being carried out under cover of darkness, as shown by the pine torches carried by their comrades. There were many carrying duties associated with the ashigaru role, but their numbers were also augmented by labourers.

ashigaru were continually replaced and their firing produced 600 or 700 dead or wounded.'

The use of the word 'replaced' suggests rotating volley fire, but a very different use of the ashigaru arquebus is contained in the following amusing extract, which is concerned with the preliminaries to the siege of Ulsan in 1597. As the actual fortress of Ulsan was still being built, many of the Japanese troops were quartered outside the walls, which is where the following incident occurred:

'Over halfway through the night of the 13th day of the 12th month a furious sound of gunfire broke out in the Nabeshima camp. Near the camp was a large swamp to which many swans came every night. When flying away at dawn they passed over the Nabeshima camp. The ashigaru had been told about this by Nabeshima, and they would·fire their arquebuses at the flying birds, bringing down one or two. This happened every night. When the sound of gunfire happened that night Yasumasa thought they were shooting swans again.'

The gunfire, however, was not the ashigaru taking potshots at the swans, but a full-scale Chinese attack. The passage continues:

'However, many troops from the Nabeshima and Chugoku contingents then came fleeing into

Yasumasa's camp. Yasumasa quickly put on his armour, seized his spear and galloped off. Eleven of his samurai were there to protect him.'

Archery squads

As the Japanese troops were not within the secure walls of a castle but in a temporary camp outside they were quickly overrun, and were eventually saved by the next group dealt with in the *Zôhyô Monogatari*: the ashigaru archery squads.

'On the matter of the disposition of the archery corps, stand one archer in the space between two matchlock men, to cover the arquebuses reloading. An arrow can be loosed in between the two matchlockmen firing, thus covering the reloading interval.'

Just as in the case of the arquebuses, the yumi ko gashira takes charge of the archers.

'When the enemy are a distance away it is important not to fire arrows from the quiver. The ko gashira who is in command will take charge of the matter, and will order the firing of arrows when the enemy are closer. The decision about the effective firing distance is a difficult one to make.'

Target priorities are again the horses:

'When the enemy advance in a dense mass divide up into right and left sections and fire. In the case of a mounted enemy fire at the horses.'

Like the arquebusiers, the archers also had to be prepared for hand to hand fighting:

'When the arrows in the quiver are running low, do not use up the last arrow, but make a line to permit firing to continue, and engage in hand to hand fighting. When forced to withdraw defend from a spear's length away, and then fire into the space. This should be completely successful. If you are forced to fire while looking up at their faces you cannot ward off an enemy. These are the secrets of bow fighting . . . The bowstring must be folded up so that it is not cut through when this is done.'

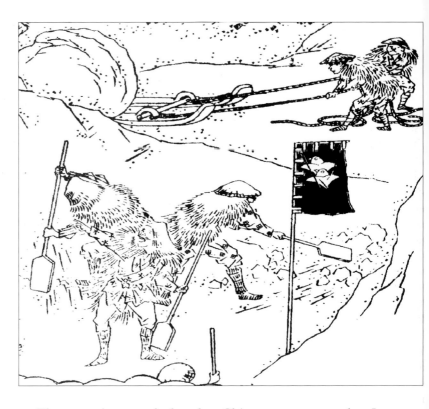

A detail from *Ehon Toyotomi Gunki* showing impressed labour being used to clear snow for an army's advance. The peasants have dressed as warmly as they could in straw capes. The flag of Shibata Katsuie is stuck into the snow as a reminder to them of who is in charge.

In this unusual illustration from *Ehon Toyotomi Gunki*, a group of ashigaru are burning a village. Such activities were rare, and this particular incident only took place as a means of denying support to a nearby enemy.

The surprise attack by the Chinese army on the Japanese encampment outside the 'building site' of Ulsan castle in 1597 was repulsed by well-trained ashigaru archers under the firm leadership of a young samurai hero:

'The enemy attacked the encampment of Môri's samurai Reizei Minbu, and in the end killed Minbu. The troops who saw this stayed in the castle, but one man among them, Yoshimi Taizô, in spite of being a youth of 18 years old, excelled in the Way of Bow and Arrow. He stood the troops under his command in a circle and, having ordered the ashigaru, "Draw the enemy near, and shoot in such a way that the arrows are not ineffective," charged into the midst of many thousands of the enemy.'

Spearmen

The final weapon group discussed in the *Zôhyô Monogatari* are the spearmen ashigaru, who had to be particularly well drilled and well disciplined, because their enormous nagae-yari pikes had the potential to cause as much trouble for friend as foe if not used correctly. Some of the most vivid lines in the *Zôhyô Monogatari* concern spear fighting. The length of the nagae-yari, and the need for the ashigaru spearmen to keep the blades even, implies the existence of some form of 'pike drill'. Using the *Zôhyô Monogatari* and other accounts, it is possible to speculate as to what this accepted system may have consisted of:

'The arquebus and bow rounds having finished, the spears are under orders. Before the fighting starts place the sheaths inside the *mune-ita* [the top of the armour breastplate]. Long scabbard-like spear sheaths must be thrust into the belt at the side.

The Korean campaigns saw many actions directed against civilians. In this illustration from *Ehon Taikô ki*, samurai and ashigaru loot a Korean village. One soldier steals a vase, another takes rolls of cloth, while a woman is the prize for a third.

'Unlike samurai spearmen, where spears are thought of as only for thrusting with, here many are of one mind, with spear points moving together, keeping a rhythm. When one or two meet it is fine to fight individually, but when spears are used en masse there must be coordination and timing, with no exception. As for spear techniques, it is believed to be a good thing to be able to knock down an enemy sashimono [literally a flag, but indicating the horseman himself]. When the enemy are mounted a quick thrust at the horse's belly will make it buck and the man will fall off.

'Line up in one rank three *shaku* apart, not thrusting but at the ready in a large row to hit the enemy. When facing an attack by horsemen line up in one rank kneeling, lie the spear down and wait. When contact is imminent lift up the spear head into the area of the horse's breast. When the point pierces the skin hold on to it! Whether you are cutting at men and horses, it may be that you will feel you are being forced to pull out the spear, and it is a general rule to stand fast to the bitter end and not throw into disorder the collaborative actions. After you have driven the enemy back, to pursue for about one *chô* is sufficient.'

The section concludes with advice on how far to stick the spear into an enemy, and a comment that the successful employment of many spears required skill, perseverance, and constant readiness. A good illustration of controlled spear work occurs in the *Ôu Eikei Gunki*, the great chronicle of the wars in the north of Japan at the time of Sekigahara. In the section on the attack on Yuzawa castle, a frontal and a flank attack are delivered simultaneously, and naginata are also used:

'Iyo Choza'emonjo Sadahira and Ichikuri Heibu Shorin with 300 men, plus the forces under Yoshida Magoichi and Nishino Shuri

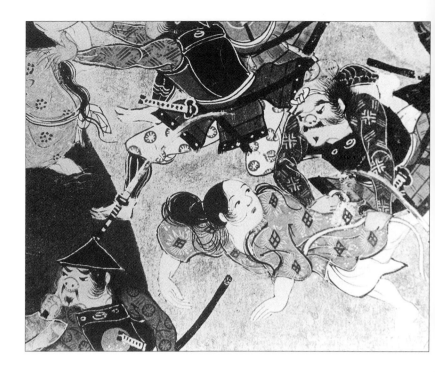

Ryôshun and Magosaburô of the same family with 500 men, arranged their spear blades in an even line and went to fight against the Yuzawa side. From the flank at the same time eighteen nagae-yari men acquired a name for themselves by advancing in one rank holding spears and naginata. They cut into all sides of the dense crowd as they surrounded the unfortunates . . . '

Spear carriers and standard bearers

Most of the ashigaru who were not attached to the disciplined weapons units would be in close attendance upon the daimyô, and here the opportunities for individual glory, and, for that matter, death, were that much greater. It was the sandal bearers and spear carriers who would willingly receive the arrows and bullets meant for their masters. One of the most dramatic scenes in the film *Kagemusha* shows the ranks of Takeda Shingen's bodyguard, among whom are many ashigaru, closing in around him to give protection during a surprise night attack.

This crude artwork, which shows an ashigaru arquebusier taking aim, illustrates how elevated sights could be used to good effect.

The most vulnerable position for an ashigaru to occupy was standard bearer in a daimyô's army. To kill an ashigaru standard bearer could be a feat akin to taking the head of a worthy samurai. In the *Momii Nikki* account of the battle of Awataguchi a certain Yata Genji earns a commendation this way:

'The general Sanshichi was jammed tight and attacked. Over 700 of his followers were crowded together. While some recovered and went back others were killed. The Flag Commissioner Tobe Shirô was cornered by the *kashira* Eta Heiko and the retainer Yata Kotairô and was killed in the press, and Yata Genji also slew the standard bearer. To a loud yell from those present he snatched away Nobuo's uma jirushi, which was in the form of a golden pestle . . . '

In the *Banshô Sayo Gunki* we read of another desperate attempt to 'keep the flag flying':

'The swift current separated those who had the flags and the uma jirushi of Ukita . . . then the flag carrier too was killed by a galloping horse as he walked along, the uma jirushi fell to the ground many times and finally had to be abandoned.'

Not surprisingly, service in the particularly dangerous role of standard bearer was likely to ensure promotion to samurai. In the *Komatsu Gunki*:

'A certain Deguchi, a retainer of Eguchi's, held Motokura Nagahide's hata jirushi [streamer-like flag], and while he had it performed feats against the rebels on many occasions . . . Eguchi recommended promotion for this and gave him a 200 koku fief . . . '

An interesting page from *Geijutsu Hiden Zue* showing how to fire in the dark on pre-selected targets using cords to gauge the elevation. A similar scene occurs in the film *Kagemusha*.

A detail from *Geijutsu Hiden Zue* showing a large calibre arquebus mounted as a cannon on wheels, c. 1850. A samurai is in charge, while the gun crew is comprised of ashigaru.

Another account is found in the *Kiyomasa-ki*:

'As the defeated army flooded out and it was realised that they were scattering in all directions, the men accompanying Kiyomasa were Shoba-yashi Shunjin, Morimoto Gidayu, Kashihara Tôgorô, Ikeda Jinshirô, Wada Takemaru, the bow carrier Mizutani Yasu no jô, the uma-jirushi carrier Yokichi, the sandal bearers Itsuho, Oyoshi, Hike and Ôe Jinshichi.'

It may first be noticed how many of these close attendants on Katô Kiyomasa have no surnames. These include the ashigaru who held Katô Kiyomasa's great standard that bore the motto of the Nichiren sect of Buddhism, 'Namu Myôho Renge Kyô' (Hail to the Lotus of the Divine Law). Because of his conduct at this battle the uma-jirushi carrier Yokichi was promoted to the status of samurai, and in the *Zokusen Kiyomasa-ki* (the second series of the Kiyomasa-ki) we can read more about him:

'[at the time of the above battle] . . . present with Kiyomasa. Kashihara Tôgorô, Katô Hiraza'emon are recorded, a certain Wada Takemaru was among them . . . As for the uma-jirushi carrier Yokichi at the time he received from Shobayashi Yo'emon a fief of 300 koku.'

Accounts of individual ashigaru glory outside the ranks of a daimyô's attendants are very rare indeed. One of the few in existence concerns how an ashigaru was inspired by the sight of a dead samurai's sashimono banner lying on the battlefield, and went on to earn great glory:

'One of their common soldiers had lost heart and retreated, but when he was about to drink water from a stream by the roadside, he saw

A postcard from the late 19th century showing the type of barracks that would have been occupied by the ashigaru ranks of a daimyô's army. None of the buildings shown has survived the fires and wars of modern Japan.

the great sashimono where it had fallen into the water. He saw the characters on it, and regretted that he had retreated. This mere ashigaru hurried back and charged into the midst of the great army of the enemy. He fought with great desperation and took three helmeted heads . . . He ended his career with 200 koku.'

The above accounts show how the successful general on the battlefield achieved loyalty and efficiency at all levels of those under his command. Every ashigaru had his place, his function and his value. The *Zôhyô Monogatari* is eloquent testimony to this, but Matsudaira notes throughout that discipline is essential, and reserves his strongest language for ashigaru who are careless with equipment:

'It is the rule that on the battlefield no equipment must be abandoned. Small spear scabbards must be placed within the mune-ita of the armour. Long scabbards must be kept at the side. Ramrods should be placed in the side like a quiver and not mislaid. It is also the rule that horses must not be allowed to wander freely. This is strictly forbidden.'

Nevertheless, the whole tone of the *Zôhyô Monogatari* is one of positive acceptance, recognising that by 1649 ashigaru were a vital part of any army, and that the resources devoted to their welfare, training and support were never wasted. By dint of edict, definition and achievement they had long since achieved the ultimate accolade that Japan's traditional warrior class could bestow. Ashigaru, who had once been no more than a peasant rabble, had become samurai.

This excellent modern depiction of the stages of firing an arquebus volley by artist Colin Upton shows the different roles of the men in the arquebus squads. The ko gashira directs the operation, the bullet carrier gives out the supply, and the arquebusiers load and fire. Spare fuses are kept on a frame at the front, and to save time in reloading the ramrod is stuck into the ground. (Reproduced from the Taikô Wargames Rules, by Flagship Games Ltd)

An ashigaru gun crew operating in a rainstorm. This picture, taken from *Geijutsu Hiden Zue*, shows the crew sheltering under a large cloth, which is held up by poles. The samurai wears a facemask.

MUSEUM COLLECTIONS

Considering how many simple suits of armour must have been produced for the ashigaru it is surprising how little seems to have been preserved. In most museums it is almost exclusively elaborate suits of samurai armour that are on show. The most dramatic exception is the Watanabe Museum in Tottori on the Japan Sea coast, which has a remarkable collection that features rank after rank of armour, including many ashigaru suits, arranged like a football terrace. There are also numerous weapons and flags. The Ii collection in Hikone is now housed in a purpose-built museum at the foot of the castle hill, and even though the exhibits are rotated, the chances are that any casual visit will yield several examples of the red devils' armour (so called because of the colour of the lacuqer). The Takeda Museum at the Erin-ji near Kôfu contains all the Takeda war banners, while the Date Museum in Sendai has several examples of their renowned bullet-proof armours.

Outside Japan few collections have ashigaru equipment. The best is undoubtedly the Royal Armouries Museum in Leeds, which has a splendid okegawa-dô armour and several arquebuses and spears. Several other museums have collections of jingasa. For good mixed displays of samurai and ashigaru equipment visit Snowshill Manor near Broadway in Worcestershire, or the Metropolitan Museum in New York.

As all museum collections are constantly changing I suggest you visit my Website (www.stephenturnbull.com) for up-to-date information.

BIBLIOGRAPHY AND FURTHER READING

The main sources for this book are two works by Yoshihiko Sasama entitled *Ashigaru no Seikatsu* (1969) and *Buke Senjin Sahô Shôsei* (1968). The first is the standard work on the history of ashigaru and contains long sections from *Zôhyô Monogatari*. The second, which is concerned with the entire samurai class, also contains much from *Zôhyô Monogatari*, and other essays and primary source material on ashigaru. The ashigaru are also covered in two recent volumes in the series *Senryaku, senjutsu, heiki jiten*. Volume 2 *Nihon Sengoku hen* includes many drawings of ashigaru in action, while volume 6 *Nihon Johaku hen* concentrates on their role in sieges. The information about the ashigaru operations in Korea is largely taken from Kuwada *et al.* (Editors) *Chôsen no Eki (Nihon no senshi Volume 5)*, which has an extensive appendix of primary source material.

Some of the primary source material referred to here may be found in translation in my book *The Samurai Sourcebook* (Cassell, 1998), while different illustrations of ashigaru equipment appear in my *Samurai Warfare* (Cassell, 1996). For a thorough case study of Nagashino, the battle that placed ashigaru on the military map of Japan, see my *Nagashino 1575* (Osprey, 2000) in the Osprey Campaigns series. My forthcoming book on the Japanese invasion of Korea (*Hunting the*

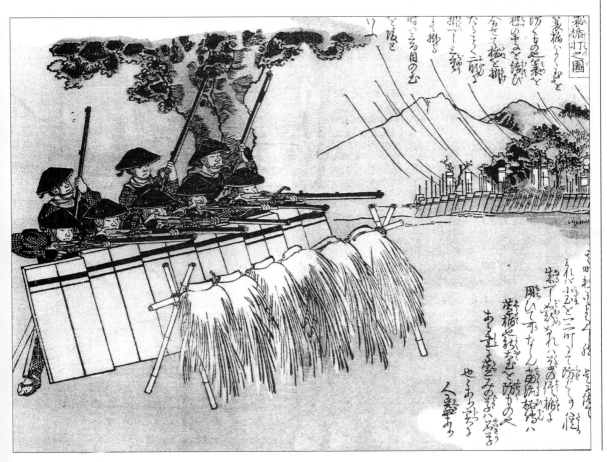

A group of arquebusiers line up behind wooden shields in this detail from *Geijutsu Hiden Zue*. The men's straw raincoats are kept close at hand, as it appears to have started to rain.

Tiger – to be published by Cassell in 2001) will contain much more material about the use of ashigaru on the battlefield.

Kurosawa's films *Kagemusha* and *Ran* give very accurate depictions of ashigaru warfare. *Throne of Blood* also shows ashigaru in action during a siege, while if you would like to try your hand at commanding armies of ashigaru then I wholeheartedly recommend the computer strategy game *Shogun: Total War* produced by Electronic Arts.

For a monthly update on matters relating to samurai and ashigaru visit my website (www.stephenturnbull.com). As well as giving details of my latest research interests and publications the site is used to review books and computer games, and to give information about museum exhibitions and public lectures on samurai.

A detail from *Ehon Toyotomi Gunki* showing spearmen and arquebusiers defending a castle. Bundles of bamboo provide protection, and the women of the garrison bring the men a welcome cup of tea.

CHRONOLOGY OF THE ASHIGARU

All dates AD

792	Collapse of Emperor Tenmu's conscription army system.
940	Footsoldiers in action during the rebellion of Taira Masakado.
1180-1392	Footsoldiers used during the Gempei Wars, and in subsequent conflicts over the next three centuries.
1467	The first use of the term 'ashigaru' for casual recruits to armies.
1530	Widespread use of disciplined ashigaru squads is recorded.
1543	Introduction of European firearms to Japan.
1575	The battle of Nagashino shows the power of organised volley firing.
1588	Hideyoshi's 'Sword Hunt' disarms the peasantry.
1591	Hideyoshi's 'Separation Edict' divides samurai and farmer, making ashigaru into lower-ranking samurai.
1592-98	Arquebus squads used to good effect in the Korean campaign.
1603	Establishment of the Tokugawa Shogunate. Ashigaru are officially recognised as of the samurai class.
1638	Shimabara Rebellion. A peasant army holds out against the Shogun's army.
1649	Publication of *Zôhyô Monogatari*, written by a commander of ashigaru.

This double page spread from *Ehon Taikôki* is an excellent depiction of ashigaru warfare. On the left ashigaru under the command of a samurai ashigaru-taishô (identified by his flag bearer) are making a sally out of a defended castle past fences of brushwood. The besiegers have let the vanguard group pass by, and have then caught the following group in a volley of arrows fired through the openings of wooden shields. We can also see groups of spearmen with spears of differing lengths, and a unit of arquebusiers at the ready. All are wearing typical ashigaru armour with conical jingasa.

THE PLATES

A: REGULAR ASHIGARU, C. 1467

Many ashigaru were drawn from a samurai's own estates, and it is one such footsoldier who is depicted in this plate. The source is a figure included on a painted scroll entitled *Shinnyodô Engi Emaki*, which is owned by the Gokuraku-ji in Kyoto and illustrates an incident during the Ônin War in 1467. On the original scroll the ashigaru is in attendance on a mounted samurai who has been sent to deal with a disturbance caused by less lawful ashigaru (those attracted by the prospect of loot), whose activities are illustrated in Plate H.

A1: Our 'regular' ashigaru wears a *haramaki* style of armour, which wrapped around the torso and opened at the back. It is fully laced in *kebiki-odoshi* (close-spaced lacing) style. The ashigaru wears *kote* (sleeve armour) and the old style of *suneate* (shinguards) which were of heavy iron plates and tied over *kaihan* (gaiters). On his feet are a pair of *tabi* (socks) and plain *waraji* (straw sandals). Helmets were not issued to foot-soldiers, so he wears an *eboshi* (stiffened cloth cap), tied on with a white *hachimaki* (headband). Units were distinguished by a small flag flown at the shoulder of the armour. He is carrying a *naginata* (glaive). At his belt he wears a *wakizashi* (short sword) together with a long *katana* (sword) slung tachi style. A spare bowstring reel is also suspended from the sword belt.

A2: The simpler *hara-ate* style of armour, which only covered the chest and groin areas, leaving the thighs and back unprotected.

A3: The *dô-maru* style of armour, shown fully spread out. It was very similar to the haramaki but opened at the side.

A4: A simple head protector made from a hachimaki to which a pad of chain mail has been sewn.

A5: An iron face-protector which tied behind the head.

A6: The *yumi* (longbow) which was of composite construction and lacquered to make it weatherproof

A7: The *ebira* (quiver) which was of woven basket-work and tied around the waist.

B: AN ASHIGARU SPEARMAN, C. 1592

By the end of the 16th century, ashigaru costume had evolved into the typical ensemble shown here.

B1: This member of a specialised *nagae yari* (long-shafted spear) unit is dressed in the characteristic red and gold armour of the Matsuura family, as would have been seen in action when they fought under Matsuura Shigenobu in Korea in 1592. His armour, which is copied from an actual specimen in the Matsuura Historical Museum on Hirado Island, is of okegawa-dô style. The breastplate and backplate, which were joined by a hinge at the left-hand side, were made from a series of horizontal iron plates riveted together and lacquered over to give a smooth surface apart from the slight ridges where the plates joined. His helmet is a simple conical iron *jingasa* (war hat) from which a cloth sunscreen hangs at the rear. His sleeve armour consists of two cloth bags to which iron plates have been sewn. His suneate are simple versions of the type worn by samurai horsemen. Through his belt are thrust a katana and a wakizashi. The *mon* (badge) of the Matsuura appears on his jingasa and on the sashimono, the identifying flag worn on the back. Round his shoulders are fastened his ration bags.

B2: The *haori* (jacket), worn on formal occasions such as parades and in winter for warmth.

B3: The water bottle made out of a section of bamboo, which would be hung from the belt.

B4: A float for crossing water. It was tied under the armpits to aid buoyancy.

B5: The wicker basket could hold other pieces of personal equipment and would be slung around the shoulders when on the march or carried with other men's baskets on a pack horse.

B6: The disposable paper 'tissues' look modern, but were used in Japan many years ago.

B7: Ashigaru who performed engineering or labouring duties would carry tools such as the handsaw, hatchet and sickle shown here.

B8: A straw mat for sleeping on.

B9: A bow almost identical to that shown in Plate A.

B10: A supply quiver for 100 arrows. These large quivers were not carried by individual archers, but were brought on to the battlefield to replenish an archer's own quivers.

C: AN ASHIGARU ARQUEBUSIER, C. 1600

A typical ashigaru arquebusier of about 1600 is shown illustrated here by one of the troops of Katô Kiyomasa. The ashigaru wears typical okegawa-dô armours.

C1: The arquebusier's jingasa is lacquered brown with the Katô 'snake's eye' mon lacquered in gold, while the breastplate of hi okegawa-dô is lacquered gold and red with '*Namu Myôho Renge Kyô*' (Hail to the Lotus of the Divine Law), the saying of Nichiren that was the Katô motto, splashed across it.

C2: A prepared cartridge, shown here in a cut-away illustration. Prepared cartridges did not make an appearance until the 17th century, and were probably introduced by the Dutch. The cartridge consists of a roll of paper containing a measured amount of gunpowder and the bullet. The cap, tied securely on to the cartridge via a ring, was withdrawn from the mouth and the contents were used. The container could then be refilled.

C3: A leather cartridge box, which would be tied at the belt. Cartridges were sometimes carried as a bandolier.

C4: A lacquered powder flask with a measuring stopper.

C5: A soft leather bullet pouch from which a bullet could be rolled out on to the metal jaws for ease of handling.

C6: A fuse coil.

C7: The storage bullet box for supplying a unit on the battlefield, used in a similar way to the large arrow quiver.

C8: The length of red lacquered bamboo acted as the 'swagger stick' for the *teppô ko gashira* (lieutenant of arquebus units) and contained a spare ramrod for use in emergencies.

C9: A powder flask for the fine-grained priming powder

At top of plate:

The stages of firing an arquebus. First, a charge of powder, measured in the cap, is poured into the barrel. This would be rammed home and followed into the barrel by the bullet from the pouch. After the final ramming the protective pan cover is swung to one side and some fine priming powder is introduced to the touch hole from the other powder flask. The cover is again closed and the burning fuse is inserted into the jaws of the serpentine. The arquebusier opens the pan cover, takes aim and pulls the trigger. The brass spring releases the serpentine which drops the smouldering match on to the powder in the pan, and the gun is fired.

D: THE CALL TO WAR, C. 1560

This plate represents a possible sequence of events involved in a call to arms by the Hôjô family, who ruled the Kanto, the area of Japan that now includes modern Tokyo.

D1: A part-time farmer and ashigaru who serves the Hôjô family is working in the fields beside his wife when a runner arrives to inform them of a muster of troops in a few days time.

D2: The ashigaru is seen re-binding the cords on the handle of his sword. He will soon be getting all his equipment together ready to march off to the assembly point.

D3: The Hôjô have been warned of a possible invasion, so these ashigaru are working in the fields with their weapons lying ready on the grass between the rice paddies. They need little else, because the nearest Hôjô satellite castle is kept well stocked with armour. They will be moving into action at a moment's notice, and are listening for the pre-arranged signal.

D4: The call is given by the *kaiyaku* (conch shell trumpeter). His master has heard the war drum from a distant castle, or has observed smoke rising from a signalling beacon, so the conch has blown for an immediate muster.

D5: An ashigaru, who was summoned into action with more time to prepare for combat, dresses in his finest clothes and prepares to eat what may be his final meal before battle. His wife looks at him sadly but proudly.

D6: On arriving at the muster station he is recorded by an official and makes a print with his index finger in ink to confirm his arrival. Many may have turned up with agricultural weapons instead of arms, but all are issued with a simple suit of armour which transforms their appearance into that of fighting men. All the ashigaru will soon be marched off to the local castle. Here they will be drilled and inspected by the samurai whose responsibility it was to supply these men for the Hôjô war effort. Once the entire local contingent was assembled a decision was made about who and how many would stay behind to strengthen the garrison, then they would set off to war as part of the full Hôjô army.

E: ASHIGARU TRAINING, C.1550

The ashigaru in this picture have been recruited from the lands owned by the Takeda family in 1550, and they are ready for the campaign that was to lead to the capture of Toishi castle from the Murakami. The men arrived at the muster station only the day before. As most of them work the fields in addition to their military service, their drill is rather rusty, so Yokota Takatoshi, who is one of the Takeda 'Twenty-Four Generals' and holds the title of ashigaru taishô, is putting them through their paces. He is particularly concerned to train them to keep their spear points level when they advance in a line three ranks deep, which is not an easy manoeuvre. His *yari kashira* (spear captains) help him to control the men as Yokota waves his war fan in exasperation. Among their equipment we see the latest okegawa-dô stencilled with the Takeda mon plus a few simple armours made by sewing lacquered plates on to a cloth backing. One wears a hara-ate. Many do not have helmets, and only a few have yet been supplied with sashimono bearing Yokota's own device. The weapons are also somewhat haphazard, and a temporary shortage of long spears has forced Yokota to make do with bamboo poles until the equipment is sorted out. The contrast between Yokota's personal ashigaru attendants and the more part-time soldiers is noticeable in demeanour as much as appearance. One old and trusted ashigaru holds Yokota's personal standard, while others carry his spear, bow and other personal arms. Yokota himself wears a green dô-maru armour complete with *haidate* (thighguards) which looks so much more substantial than the ashigaru armour. As the Takeda were one of the most professional military organisations in Japan, it would not be long before this motley crew transformed into a successful band of soldiers. In fact the 1550 campaign was a success for the Takeda. Toishi castle was captured, but Yokota Takatoshi was sadly killed in action. The source for this plate is a contemporary painting of Yokota Takatoshi and various contemporary illustrations of Takeda ashigaru on painted screens.

F: CAMPAIGN LIFE, NORTHERN JAPAN, 1591

Dramatic details of ashigaru campaign life are shown in this scene set during Hideyoshi's final operation on the Japanese mainland in 1591. Troops under Gamô Ujisato are moving against Kunoe Masazane in Kunoe in northern Japan, and things are not going well. It has been a long march up into the unfamiliar and threatening mountains. The men are all

RIGHT **An illustration from a modern Japanese comic book by Junko Miki. The picture shows the steady but rapid advance of ashigaru across ricefields. The dramatic effect is considerable.**

exhausted and tired to the point of disillusionment. One ashigaru has been bitten by an adder, and receives the recommended treatment for snake bite by having gunpowder exploded on the wound.

A miserable group of ashigaru behind him experience diarrhoea and vomiting arising from a successful attempt by the enemy to poison a well. One is suddenly sick into his helmet. Others wait to have surgery performed on horrific flesh wounds. One has an arrowhead in his cheek. Another has a broken arrow sticking out of his eye socket. He is dying, and little can be done for him. The ashigaru are all wearing identical okegawa-dô armours lacquered black. The golden mon of a hat which is the badge of the Gamô is stencilled onto their breastplates and their jingasa.

G: CAMPAIGN LIFE DURING THE SHIMABARA REBELLION, 1638

In contrast to the previous plate, the ashigaru of Matsudaira are experiencing a campaign where everything appears to be going well. These ashigaru are in action on behalf of the Tokugawa Shogun, and their mission is to quell the Christian Shimabara Rebellion at Hara in 1638. We see here the troops of Matsudaira Nobutsuna, who eventually captured Hara and whose son Nobuoki went on to write the guide to ashigaru warfare called Zôhyô Monogatari in 1649. Lord Matsudaira is wearing a fine suit of armour set off by a golden jinbaori (surcoat). Behind him are the portable signalling devices of drum, bell and horagai (conch shell trumpet). The drum is carried in a frame on a man's back, and will be beaten by a companion. All the Matsudaira ashigaru are smartly dressed in the costumes shown in an illustrated edition of Zohyo Monogatari. Their armour is lacquered black and has gold decoration and mon for identification.

In the foreground other ashigaru prepare to cross a river without damaging their equipment. They first tie up the skirts of their armour using their belts. The cartridge boxes are taken from the belt and tied high under their chins. The swords are hung round the shoulders and the arquebuses are held well clear of the water. Some have floats to help them, either the device shown in Plate B, or flat wooden boards.

The ashigaru in charge of the light artillery float the barrel of their small cannon across a river on a raft, as they do for the ammunition box, which is securely tied in place. The source for the plate is Zôhyô Monogatari and a series of drawings of a river crossing by ashigaru in the book of 1855 entitled Geijutsu Hiden Zue, illustrated by the famous artist Kuniyoshi, in the collection of the Royal Armouries Museum, Leeds.

H: ASHIGARU LOOTING DURING THE ÔNIN WAR, 1467

The other variety of troops to be called ashigaru are seen in this plate which illustrates a scene during the Ônin War in 1467. The source is the same painted scroll entitled Shinnyodô Engi Emaki which was used for Plate A, but what a contrast there is between the two types of ashigaru depicted therein. In typical fashion, this collection of ne'er-do-wells, who owe allegiance to no one but themselves, are looting houses and stores in Kyoto. They are rough characters, and have been helping themselves to looted sake. They first attached themselves to an army (whose it was they neither knew nor cared) during a recent raid, and have now slipped away from the main scene of the fighting to collect their reward in the form of unauthorised pillage. Their equipment has been picked up from previous battlefields. Only one has any armour. It is already blood-stained and damaged, and the silk cords lacing the parts together are now so heavily cut so that the whole ensemble is falling to pieces. The others appear to be wearing only a short kimono, a loincloth and a headband. Spears are used as levers to prise up floorboards in search of hidden treasures, while outside their more inebriated companions scatter documents and carry off strongboxes.

I: ASHIGARU OPERATING CATAPULT ARTILLERY, 1468

It is 1468, and these ashigaru are operating catapult artillery during the Ônin War on behalf of the Hosokawa. These are not casual troops; in times of peace they would work on the Hosokawa estates like the ashigaru shown in plate A, so they are naturally loyal, if poorly trained. The cohesive nature of

LEFT **This detail from *Ehon Toyotomi Gunki* showing the siege of Inuyama in 1584 gives a rare glimpse of ordered ashigaru ranks in action. Arquebuses are fired and spears dropped to the horizontal as the spearmen advance. The enemy front line stand ready with spears held vertically.**

RIGHT **Detail from the first Japanese arquebus firing in the UK, which took place in February 2000 as part of the regular programme of interpretations held at the Royal Armouries, Leeds. The pan is primed by Ian Bottomley, who is the Senior Curator in the Oriental Department.**

their employment is an asset for the task to which they have been allotted, which is to launch delayed action firebombs by catapult, a task requiring both discipline and timing. Such men would have to supply their own armour and equipment. For the job of pulling on catapult ropes, however, armour would get in the way, so they have abandoned it for now. Pulling simultaneously on long ropes on a Chinese-style catapult, they fling large soft-cased fireball bombs into the Yamana lines under the eagle eyes of a samurai guard and a footsoldier. Another man, who probably supervised the making of the bomb, drags a fireball into position for it to be loaded and the fuse lit.

This plate is based on detailed contemporary descriptions of such operations, with a number of assumptions being made. Medieval illustrations of the use of traction trebuchets in Europe suggest that the crew pulled the ropes vertically downwards to launch a projectile. By contrast, Chinese illustrations usually show a very large number of ropes, which would have been impracticable unless the hauliers stood away from the machine and pulled in a roughly horizontal direction. This is the arrangement deemed appropriate for this reconstruction. The other assumption is that a man would have given tension to the sling by holding on to the projectile until the last moment, hence the extra operatives shown here.

J: ASHIGARU SPEARMEN CLASH AT ODAWARA, 1590

The final evolution of ashigaru into disciplined troops fighting as a coordinated group is illustrated by a fierce fight between two rivals groups of spearmen. The scene is one of the attacks made on the fortress of Odawara during the great siege of 1590. The 'red devils' of Ii Naomasa are taking on their equivalents in the Hôjô family in hand-to-hand fighting, which is carried out enthusiastically as a rare break in the boredom of the long siege. The engagement is fought over the rubble from the collapsed wall, which had been loosened by mining during the night, and the uneven ground has broken up what was a steady advance. It is now every man for himself. Both sides show a highly developed style of ashigaru armour, which is based around the very practical okegawa-dô. The Ii troops wear identically coloured bright red lacquered armour, and only the jingasa make them look any different from samurai. We see the nobori banners bearing the name of Hachiman Dai Bosatsu, the Japanese god of war. The Hôjô are dressed in black, with their mon of a fish-scale design. The armour is copied from actual specimens in the Ii Historical Museum, Hikone and the Kanazawa Prefectural Museum respectively.

GLOSSARY

ashigaru kashira	Captain of foot soldiers
ashigaru ko gashira	Lieutenant of foot soldiers
ashigaru taishô	General of foot soldiers
chô	A distance of 109m
daimyô	Feudal lord
dô	Body armour
dô maru	Style of armour wrapping round the body and fastening at the side
ebira	Quiver
eboshi	Stiffened cap
genin	Samurai attendant
gô	Measure of .18 litres
go uma mawari	Mounted bodyguard
hachimaki	Head band
haidate	Thigh guards
haori	Jacket
hara-ate	Armour for upper body and groin only
hara kiri	Ritual suicide
haramaki	Style of armour wrapping round the body and opening at the rear
horagai	Conch shell trumpet
jinbaori	Samurai's surcoat
jingasa	Foot soldier's light helmet
kaihan	Cloth gaiters
kaiyaku	Conch shell trumpeter
kashira	Officer of ashigaru
katana	Long sword
kebiki odoshi	Close spaced lacing of armour
ken	Length of 1.8m
kimono	Garment like a dressing gown
ko uma jirushi	Smaller of a lord's standards
koku	Measure of 180 litres
kote	Sleeve armour
kusazuri	Skirts of armour
mon	Heraldic badge
monme	Weight of 3.75gms
mune ita	Upper section of breastplate
nagae yari	Long-shafted spear
naginata	Glaive
nobori	Vertical banner
o uma jirushi	Larger of a lord's standards
okashi gusoku	Loan armour provided for ashigaru
okegawa-dô	Smooth surfaced armour for ashigaru
sashimono	Flag worn on the back of armour
Sengoku jidai	Period of Warring States (1467-1600)
shaku	Length of 30.3cms
shashu no ashigaru	Archer foot soldiers in the 14th century
suneate	Shinguards
tabi	Socks
tachi	Long sword worn slung from a belt
teppô ko gashira	Officer in charge of arquebusiers
tsukai ban	Messenger corps
uma jirushi	Standard used by samurai
wakizashi	Short sword
waraji	Straw sandals
yari	Spear
yari kashira	Captain of spears
yumi kashira	Captain of bows
zori tori	Sandal bearer, equivalent to a batman

INDEX